AMERICAN POLITICAL, ECONOMIC, AND SECURITY ISSUES

THE 2010 CENSUS: OPERATIONS AND OUTCOMES

AMERICAN POLITICAL, ECONOMIC, AND SECURITY ISSUES

Additional books in this series can be found on Nova's website under the Series tab.

Additional E-books in this series can be found on Nova's website under the E-book tab.

SOCIAL ISSUES, JUSTICE AND STATUS

Additional books in this series can be found on Nova's website under the Series tab.

Additional E-books in this series can be found on Nova's website under the E-book tab.

AMERICAN POLITICAL, ECONOMIC, AND SECURITY ISSUES

THE 2010 CENSUS: OPERATIONS AND OUTCOMES

KATHERINE M. DE LUCA
AND
CECILIA F. MORETTI
EDITORS

Nova Science Publishers, Inc.
New York

Copyright © 2011 by Nova Science Publishers, Inc.

All rights reserved. No part of this book may be reproduced, stored in a retrieval system or transmitted in any form or by any means: electronic, electrostatic, magnetic, tape, mechanical photocopying, recording or otherwise without the written permission of the Publisher.

For permission to use material from this book please contact us:
Telephone 631-231-7269; Fax 631-231-8175
Web Site: http://www.novapublishers.com

NOTICE TO THE READER

The Publisher has taken reasonable care in the preparation of this book, but makes no expressed or implied warranty of any kind and assumes no responsibility for any errors or omissions. No liability is assumed for incidental or consequential damages in connection with or arising out of information contained in this book. The Publisher shall not be liable for any special, consequential, or exemplary damages resulting, in whole or in part, from the readers' use of, or reliance upon, this material. Any parts of this book based on government reports are so indicated and copyright is claimed for those parts to the extent applicable to compilations of such works.

Independent verification should be sought for any data, advice or recommendations contained in this book. In addition, no responsibility is assumed by the publisher for any injury and/or damage to persons or property arising from any methods, products, instructions, ideas or otherwise contained in this publication.

This publication is designed to provide accurate and authoritative information with regard to the subject matter covered herein. It is sold with the clear understanding that the Publisher is not engaged in rendering legal or any other professional services. If legal or any other expert assistance is required, the services of a competent person should be sought. FROM A DECLARATION OF PARTICIPANTS JOINTLY ADOPTED BY A COMMITTEE OF THE AMERICAN BAR ASSOCIATION AND A COMMITTEE OF PUBLISHERS.

Additional color graphics may be available in the e-book version of this book.

Library of Congress Cataloging-in-Publication Data

The 2010 census : operations and outcomes / editors, Katherine M. De Luca and Cecilia F. Moretti.
  p. cm.
  Includes bibliographical references and index.
  ISBN 978-1-61324-348-0 (hardcover : alk. paper) 1. United States--Census, 23rd, 2010--Evaluation. 2. United States--Census, 23rd, 2010--Methodology. I. Luca, Katherine M. De. II. Moretti, Cecilia.
  HA201.14.A33 2011
  317.3--dc22
                              2011012563

Published by Nova Science Publishers, Inc. † New York

Contents

Preface		**vii**
Chapter 1	The 2010 Decennial Census: Background and Issues *Jennifer D. Williams*	1
Chapter 2	2010 Census: Data Collection Operations Were Generally Completed as Planned, but Long-standing Challenges Suggest Need for Fundamental Reforms *United States Government Accountability Office*	31
Chapter 3	2010 Census: Key Efforts to Include Hard-to-Count Populations Went Generally as Planned; Improvements Could Make the Efforts More Effective for Next Census *United States Government Accountability Office*	73
Chapter 4	2010 Census: Follow-up Should Reduce Coverage Errors, but Effects on Demographic Groups Need to Be Determined *United States Government Accountability Office*	111
Chapter 5	2010 Census: Cooperation with Enumerators Is Critical to a Successful Headcount *United States Government Accountability Office*	129
Chapter 6	2010 Census: Plans for Census Coverage Measurement Are on Track, but Additional Steps Will Improve Its Usefulness *United States Government Accountability Office*	145
Index		**163**

PREFACE

The Bureau of the Census Director's constitutional mandate to enumerate the U.S. population every 10 years has been summarized with deceptive simplicity: count each person whose usual residence is in the United States; count the person only once and count him or her at the right location. In reality, the attempt to find all U.S. residents and correctly enumerate them is increasingly complicated, expensive and it attracts congressional scrutiny. This book discusses the major innovations that were planned for the 2010 census; problems encountered, issues of census accuracy, coverage and fairness and the present status of census operations.

Chapter 1 - The 23rd decennial census of the U.S. population began on January 25, 2010, in Noorvik, AK, where the Bureau of the Census Director, among others, traveled by snowmobile and dogsled to enumerate the residents. Most U.S. households—about 120 million—received their census forms by mail in March, ahead of the official April 1 Census Day, and 74% of the households that received forms mailed them back. From May through July, the Census Bureau contacted about 47 million nonresponding households and on December 21, 2010, released the official state population figures and total U.S. resident population of 308,745,538 as of Census Day.

Chapter 2 - Although the U.S. Census Bureau (Bureau) generally completed the field data collection phase of the 2010 Census consistent with its operational plans, at $13 billion, 2010 was the costliest census in the nation's history. Moving forward, it will be important to both refine existing operations as well as to reexamine the fundamental approach to the census to better address longstanding issues such as securing participation and escalating costs. As requested, this report reviews (1) the conduct of nonresponse follow-up (NRFU), where enumerators collect data from households that did not return their census forms, (2) the implementation of other field operations critical to a complete count, and (3) potential reexamination areas that could help produce a more cost-effective 2020 Census. The report is based on GAO's analysis of Bureau data and documents, surveys of local census office managers, and field observations.

Chapter 3 - To overcome the long-standing challenge of enumerating hard-tocount (HTC) groups such as minorities and renters, the U.S. Census Bureau (Bureau), used outreach programs, such as paid advertising, and partnered with thousands of organizations to enlist their support for the census. The Bureau also conducted Service-Based Enumeration (SBE), which was designed to count people who frequent soup kitchens or other service providers, and the Be Counted/Questionnaire Assistance Center (QAC) program, designed to count individuals who believed the census had missed them. As requested, GAO assessed how the design of these efforts compared to 2000 and the extent to which they were implemented as planned. GAO reviewed Bureau budget, planning, operational, and evaluation documents; observed enumeration efforts in 12 HTC areas; surveyed local census office managers; and interviewed Bureau officials.

Chapter 4 - The U.S. Census Bureau (Bureau) puts forth tremendous effort to conduct a complete and accurate count of the nation's population and housing; yet some degree of error in the form of persons missed, duplicated, or counted in the wrong place is inevitable due to the complexity in counting a large and diverse population. The Bureau designed two operations, Coverage Follow-up (CFU) and Field Verification (FV), to reduce certain types of counting, or coverage, errors in the 2010 Census. GAO was asked to assess (1) the extent to which the Bureau completed CFU and FV on schedule and within estimated cost and (2) the implications of their key design elements for improving coverage.

GAO reviewed Bureau evaluations, planning, and other documents on CFU and FV, and prior GAO work, and interviewed Bureau officials.

Chapter 5 - On May 1, 2010, the U.S. Census Bureau (Bureau) will launch its massive follow-up effort with the roughly 48 million households that did not mail back their census forms (130 million forms were delivered). As part of this nonresponse follow-up effort, over 600,000 enumerators will fan out across the country, personally contacting nonresponding housing units as many as six times in an effort to ensure everyone is counted.

As requested, GAO's testimony in Los Angeles (L.A.) focuses on the importance of census participation, paying particular attention to (1) the Bureau's preparedness for nonresponse follow-up in terms of workload and staffing levels, (2) why it will be critical for Angelenos and others across the country to cooperate with enumerators during nonresponse follow-up, and (3) key steps the Bureau needs to take moving forward to ensure nonresponse follow-up is timely and accurate. The testimony is based on previously issued and ongoing GAO work.

Chapter 6- Assessing the accuracy of the census is essential given that census data are used to apportion seats in Congress, to redraw congressional districts, and for many other public and private purposes. The U.S. Census Bureau's (Bureau) Census Coverage Measurement program (CCM) is to assess the accuracy of the 2010 Census and improve the design of operations for the 2020 Census. In April 2008, GAO recommended that the Bureau identify how it would relate CCM results—where the 2010 Census was accurate and inaccurate—to census operations to improve future censuses. Knowing where the 2010 Census was inaccurate can help inform research to improve the 2020 Census.

GAO was asked to examine (1) the status of CCM planning and (2) the effects of design decisions since GAO issued its April 2008 report. GAO reviewed Bureau documents related to CCM design and National Academy of Sciences reports, and interviewed responsible Bureau officials.

In: The 2010 Census: Operations and Outcomes ISBN: 978-1-61324-348-0
Editors: K. De Luca and C. Moretti   © 2011 Nova Science Publishers, Inc.

Chapter 1

THE 2010 DECENNIAL CENSUS: BACKGROUND AND ISSUES[*]

Jennifer D. Williams

SUMMARY

The 23rd decennial census of the U.S. population began on January 25, 2010, in Noorvik, AK, where the Bureau of the Census Director, among others, traveled by snowmobile and dogsled to enumerate the residents. Most U.S. households—about 120 million—received their census forms by mail in March, ahead of the official April 1 Census Day, and 74% of the households that received forms mailed them back. From May through July, the Census Bureau contacted about 47 million nonresponding households and on December 21, 2010, released the official state population figures and total U.S. resident population of 308,745,538 as of Census Day.

The Bureau's constitutional mandate to enumerate the U.S. population every 10 years has been summarized with deceptive simplicity: count each person whose usual residence is in the United States; count the person only once; and count him or her at the right location. In reality, the attempt to find all U.S. residents and correctly enumerate them is increasingly complicated and expensive, and attracts congressional scrutiny. This report discusses the major innovations that

---

[*] This is an edited, reformatted and augmented version of Congressional Research Services publication R40551, dated February 3, 2011.

were planned for 2010; problems encountered; issues of census accuracy, coverage, and fairness; and the present status of census operations.

For 2010, the Bureau devised a short-form questionnaire that asked for the age, sex, race, and ethnicity (Hispanic or non-Hispanic) of each household resident, his or her relationship to the person filling out the form, and whether the housing unit was rented or owned by a member of the household. The census long form, which for decades collected detailed socioeconomic and housing data from a sample of the population, was replaced by the American Community Survey, an ongoing survey of about 250,000 households per month that gathers largely the same data as its predecessor.

Another innovation for 2010 was to have been the development of highly specialized handheld computers to automate two essential census field operations: address canvassing and nonresponse follow-up (NRFU). The goal of pre-census address canvassing was to verify and correct census maps and addresses for mailing census forms and sending enumerators. During NRFU, census workers tried repeatedly to visit or telephone people who had not completed their questionnaires and obtain information from them. Testing had revealed such serious problems with the handheld devices that although the Bureau used them for address canvassing, it resorted to the traditional paper-based approach for NRFU. The change required the Bureau to hire and train more NRFU staff, at increased expense. In 2009, the total life-cycle cost of the 2010 census was projected at $14.7 billion, instead of the previously estimated $11.5 billion. The problems with the handhelds fueled concerns that the success of the census could be at risk. Some feared, in particular, that the late-date changes to NRFU could impair census accuracy, reduce coverage, and exacerbate the recurrent likelihood of differential undercount—the greater tendency for minorities and less affluent members of society than for Whites and wealthier people to be undercounted.

Part of the Bureau's effort to maximize census accuracy and coverage was a communications strategy built on paid advertising, Bureau partnerships with local governments and other organizations, and the Census in Schools program. In addition, the Bureau made questionnaires accessible to people lacking English proficiency or having visual or hearing limitations.

INTRODUCTION

The U.S. Constitution—Article 1, Section 2, clause 3, as modified by Section 2 of the Fourteenth Amendment—requires a population census every 10 years, to serve as the basis for apportioning seats in the House of

Representatives. Decennial census data also are used for within-state redistricting and in certain formulas that determine the annual distribution of more than $400 billion dollars in federal and state funds.[1] Census numbers, moreover, are the foundation for constructing national and state estimates of current population size and projections of future size.[2] The Constitution stipulates that the enumeration is to be conducted "in such Manner as they [Congress] shall by Law direct." Congress, through Title 13 of the *United States Code*, has delegated this responsibility to the Secretary of Commerce and, within the Department of Commerce (DOC), the Bureau of the Census. Both the Commerce Secretary and the Census Bureau Director are appointed by the President, by and with the advice and consent of the Senate.

The Census Bureau's task in conducting the once-a-decade enumeration has been summarized very simply: count each person whose usual residence is in the United States; count that person only once; and count him or her at the right location, where the person lives all or most of the time.[3] Far from being simple, however, the attempt to find and correctly enumerate 100% of U.S. residents is increasingly complicated and expensive, even though Title 13 U.S.C., Section 221, requires compliance with the census and provides for a fine of up to $100 for nonresponse. In accordance with provisions of the Sentencing Reform Act of 1984, Title 18 U.S.C., Sections 3559 and 3571, the possible fine has been adjusted to not more than $5,000. This report discusses the major innovations that were planned for the 2010 census, problems encountered with the attempt to automate certain census field operations, the persistent differential census undercount of less advantaged groups in the population, efforts to ensure an equitable census, and the present status of census operations.

As *Table 1* shows, many key census activities already have occurred, and the rest will follow in 2011. The 23rd census began north of the Arctic Circle on January 25, 2010, in Noorvik, AK, where the Bureau Director, among others, traveled by snowmobile and dogsled to enumerate the residents.[4] Most U.S. households—about 120 million—received their census forms by mail in March,[5] ahead of the official April 1 Census Day, and 74% of the households that received forms mailed them back.[6] From May through July, about 565,000 census takers[7] contacted approximately 47 million households that either did not receive a questionnaire or did not answer and return it.[8] On December 21, 2010, 10 days before the legal deadline, the Bureau released the official state population figures for House apportionment and the total U.S. resident population of 308,745,538 as of Census Day.[9]

Table 1. Timeline for the 2010 Census

Date	Action
January 2008	The Bureau opened regional 2010 census offices.
Fall 2008	Recruitment began for workers to staff "early" local census offices.
Spring through Mid-Summer 2009	Census field workers completed address canvassing nationwide to update census maps and verify addresses for delivering census questionnaires and contacting nonrespondents.
Fall 2009	The Bureau opened the remaining local census offices and began recruiting enumerators needed for the peak census workload in 2010.
March 2010	Most U.S. households received their census forms by mail.
April 1, 2010	Census Day arrived.
May through July 2010	Census enumerators conducted nonresponse follow-up.
September through December 2010	Regional and local census offices closed.
December 31, 2010	By this deadline, the Bureau had to transmit to the President the official state population counts for House apportionment.
March 31, 2011	The Bureau must finish delivering redistricting data to the states.
April through December 2011	The Bureau is to produce and deliver other 2010 census data products.

Sources: Adapted from U.S. Bureau of the Census, "Interactive Timeline," http://2010.census.gov/2010census/about/timeline-flash.php, and unpublished information from the Bureau.

THE SHORT-FORM-ONLY CENSUS AND THE AMERICAN COMMUNITY SURVEY

A brief overview of modern census-taking shows how the Bureau has collected the decennial data from 1940 onward. In that year, for the first time, the census questionnaire contained 16 supplementary questions asked of a 5% sample of the population.[10] Sampling continued to be done in conjunction with the 1950 through 2000 censuses, and in 1970 the census became primarily a mail-out, mail-back operation.[11] In 2000, for example, the Bureau sent a set of basic questions on a short form to most housing units; a sample of units—

about 17%—received a long form containing these questions and others designed to gather socioeconomic and housing data for various legislative and program purposes. The forms were delivered to housing units on the Bureau's address list, with instructions that respondents were to complete and return them.[12]

Departing from recent enumerations, the 2010 census questionnaire was a short form only. It asked for the age, sex, race, and ethnicity (Hispanic or non-Hispanic) of each person in a household, as well as the individual's relationship to the person filling out the form. The form also included a question about tenure, that is, whether the housing unit was rented or owned by a member of the household.[13]

The long form was replaced by the American Community Survey (ACS), an ongoing survey of about 250,000 households per month that, with few exceptions, gathers the same data as its predecessor. The Bureau highlights the more timely availability of information as a key benefit of the ACS.[14] It provides annual data for areas with populations of at least 65,000 people, including the total United States, all states and the District of Columbia, all congressional districts, about 800 counties, and 500 metropolitan and micropolitan statistical areas. For less populous areas, the Bureau is producing multi-year averages based on ACS data collected over several years. In 2008, the Bureau released the first three-year averages for areas with 20,000 or more people, and on December 14, 2010, five-year averages became available for areas with fewer than 20,000 people.[15]

AUTOMATED FIELD OPERATIONS

Another innovation for 2010 was to have been the automation of two major census field operations: address canvassing and nonresponse follow-up (NRFU). The goal of pre-census address canvassing was for temporary Bureau field staff to verify and correct census addresses and maps, technically called the "Master Address File" (MAF) and "Topologically Integrated Geographic Encoding and Referencing" (TIGER) system. An accurate MAF/TIGER was essential for directing the census forms to the right housing units and successfully conducting nonresponse follow-up. Indeed, as the Bureau has noted, "MAF/TIGER is the foundation of the Census—it creates the universe for all other operations that collect information from the public."[16] NRFU required that enumerators try repeatedly to visit or telephone people who had not completed their census questionnaires and convince them to respond.

Because of the problems discussed below, only address canvassing was automated; NRFU was not.

Problems Encountered

As part of its 2010 census preparations, the Bureau contracted with the Harris Corporation for Field Data Collection Automation (FDCA). The objective was the development of highly specialized handheld computers to automate address canvassing and update maps with global positioning software, as well as conduct nonresponse follow-up. Testing eventually revealed significant flaws in the handhelds, such as slow operation, memory problems, and a tendency to lock up when users entered large quantities of data.[17] In April 3, 2008, congressional testimony, then-Bureau Director Steve Murdock acknowledged that the Bureau had abandoned the plan to use the handhelds for NRFU, would resort to the traditional paper-based approach, and would rely on the handhelds only for address canvassing.[18] The change required the Bureau to hire and train more NRFU staff, at increased expense.[19] The Government Accountability Office (GAO) testified to Congress in mid-2008 that the Bureau had reestimated the total life-cycle cost of the 2010 census at between $13.7 billion and $14.5 billion, instead of the previously estimated $11.5 billion.[20] A 2009 House Committee on Appropriations report raised the estimate to $14.7 billion,[21] where it remained in March 2010. NRFU was expected to account for about $2.3 billion of the $14.7 billion.[22]

Early Assessments by the DOC Inspector General and GAO

On November 18, 2008, the Commerce Department's Office of Inspector General (OIG) issued a report that identified the top management challenges DOC faced as it prepared for the transition to a new President and new Commerce Secretary. Heading the list was the need to "overcome the setbacks experienced in reengineering decennial processes and conduct a successful 2010 Census." The failure of the handhelds was prominent among the setbacks noted. According to the report, the Bureau "originally intended to develop the handhelds in-house and tested prototypes in ... 2004 and 2006. The devices had serious problems in both tests," which, in the OIG's view, "should have better informed the Bureau's efforts to define requirements."[23] The decision to contract for FDCA came "too late in the decade ... to meet ambitious fixed deadlines for the dress rehearsal tests starting in 2007 and decennial operations starting in 2009." Not until January 2008, almost two years after awarding the contract, did the Bureau deliver "a first draft of a complete, user-validated set of requirements for the handhelds and supporting infrastructure."[24] By then, the MITRE Corporation, which periodically advised the Bureau about its information technology (IT) programs for the 2010 census, had found that

> FDCA is in serious trouble. It is not clear the system will meet Census' operational needs and quality goals. The final cost is unpredictable. Immediate, significant changes are required to rescue the program. However, the risks are so large considering the available time that we recommend immediate development of contingency plans to revert to paper operations.[25]

The OIG report acknowledged that the Bureau had taken important actions, such as management changes and better oversight, to address these problems, but stated that "significant risks remain for the 2010 decennial."[26]

Similarly, the Government Accountability Office pointed out vulnerabilities in the Bureau's management of its information technology systems, including the handheld computers.[27] In a November 6, 2008, press release to announce its presidential transition website, GAO included the upcoming census among its 13 "urgent issues ... needing the attention of [then-] President-Elect Obama and the 111th Congress during the transition and the first year of the new administration and Congress."[28] The 2010 census, in large part because of IT problems and a yetto-be-determined, but substantial, total cost, remained one of the areas GAO designated as "high risk" in a January 2009 update of its high-risk series.[29] Among the concerns GAO noted in a March 2009 report were the following:

> The Dress Rehearsal[30] was originally conceived to provide a comprehensive end-to-end test of key 2010 census operations; however, ... because of the problems encountered with the handheld devices, among other things, testing was curtailed. As a result, although several critical operations underwent end-to-end testing in the Dress Rehearsal, others did not. According to the Associate Director for the 2010 census, the Bureau tested approximately 23 of 44 key operations during the Dress Rehearsal. Examples of key operations that underwent end-to-end testing ... are address canvassing and group quarters validation.[31] An example of

a key operation that was not tested is the largest field operation—nonresponse follow-up....

In December 2008, after additional development and improvements to the handheld computers, the Bureau conducted a limited field test for address canvassing, intended to assess software functionality in an operational environment. We observed this test and determined that users were generally satisfied with the performance of the handhelds.... However, the test ... included only a limited subset of functionality to be used during the 2009 address canvassing operations.[32]

GAO further observed that although nonresponse follow-up was paper based in previous censuses, the paper-based NRFU in 2010 would rely on "newly developed systems" that had "not yet been fully tested in a census-like environment.... Any significant change to an existing IT system introduces the risk that the system may not work as intended; therefore, testing all systems after changes have been made ... is critical to the success of the 2010 census."[33] GAO noted that testing had "only recently started" for the 2010 NRFU,[34] including the IT systems and infrastructure necessary to support this operation and certain other activities, such as group-quarters enumeration.[35]

THEIR ASSESSMENTS IN 2010

As nonresponse follow-up was about to begin, the Commerce Department's OIG again identified "serious issues" facing the Bureau:[36]

> Much of the ... plan is on track, but the success of NRFU—which is critical—hinges on how effectively Census controls the enormous NRFU workload and workforce.... [I]t must do so using a Paper-Based Operations Control System (PBOCS) with less functionality than planned and currently experiencing significant performance problems. PBOCS is essential for efficiently making assignments to enumerators, tracking enumeration forms, and reporting on the status of operations. And Census must recruit, hire, and pay its massive temporary workforce with a Decennial Applicant, Personnel, and Payroll System (DAPPS) also experiencing persistent performance limitations.[37]

In late March 2010, GAO, too, expressed reservations about the Bureau's IT systems, especially DAPPS and PBOCS. GAO called them "the most significant risk jeopardizing the cost and quality of the enumeration. ... Indeed, neither system has yet demonstrated the ability to function reliably under full operational loads."[38] Since December 2009, GAO noted, the Bureau had "completed many steps to improve DAPPS performance," and more were planned. The system still, however, was "experiencing capacity limitations and slow response ... even though approximately 100,000 temporary employees were ... being paid using the system versus the more than 600,000" who would require payment "at the peak of field operations."[39] With respect to PBOCS, continued GAO, early releases in January and February 2010 had "known defects, such as limited functionality, slow performance, and problems generating certain progress and performance reports."[40] Moreover, testing for "the component of the second release that will be used to manage NRFU" was incomplete as of mid-March. The third PBOCS release had to be developed and tested before being "ready for later field operations," among them "the final check of housing unit status (known as field verification), scheduled to begin in August 2010."[41]

At the end of April, GAO reiterated that "the reliability of the Bureau's automated systems, and in particular an information technology ... system used for managing the Bureau's field operations, is an open question.... The Bureau has taken steps to mitigate the risks posed by the unreliable IT systems, including upgrading hardware and software, but time will tell whether they will be able to perform as needed under full operational loads."[42]

In a December 2010 report, GAO revisited the performance of PBOCS, observing that "despite efforts to upgrade its hardware and software, PBOCS continued to experience system outages, slow performance, and problems generating and maintaining timely progress reports" at the beginning of nonresponse follow-up. The Bureau attributed these problems, GAO continued, "in part, to the compressed development and testing schedule, as well as to inadequate performance and interface testing."[43] The problems led to a backlog of census questionnaires in local census offices, and impaired the Bureau's ability to monitor NRFU workers' productivity and the quality of their interviews.[44]

CENSUS ACCURACY AND COVERAGE

As noted at the beginning of this report, the idealized expectation that the decennial census should count every person once, only once, and in the right place is deceptively simple. In reality, the task is immense and a perfect count elusive. The failure of the handhelds for nonresponse follow-up fueled concerns, like those of the Commerce Department OIG and GAO cited above, that the late-date alterations to NRFU could threaten the success of the 2010 census.

The attempt to achieve complete, accurate population coverage is challenging not only because the U.S. population is large, tends to be mobile, and is distributed over a wide geographic area, but also because the population is increasingly heterogeneous. Many households consist of racial and ethnic minorities; multiple families; low-income people; inner-city residents; those whose living circumstances are atypical; international migrants to the United States who may lack English language proficiency, lack legal status in this country, or distrust all governmental activities; or various combinations of these attributes. Any of them can make enumeration difficult, and some of them contribute markedly to the recurrent undercount of racial and ethnic minorities.

An overcount of some groups within the population can occur to the extent that the Bureau receives multiple census forms from the same people or households, then does not capture and eliminate the duplications. A husband and wife, for example, might own a vacation home and fill out a questionnaire there as well as at their usual residence. Another example would be parents who erroneously list a child on the form for their household, when the child actually is away at college and, in accordance with census residence rules, has been correctly enumerated there.

The greater tendency for minorities and less affluent members of society than for Whites and wealthier people to be undercounted leads to differential undercounts of the former. Differential undercounts are a recurrent problem in the decennial census and can diminish the perception that the count is equitable to the entire population.

Estimates of Census Coverage from Demographic Analysis

Following the 1940 census, "Census Bureau statisticians and academic researchers refined a statistical technique known as Demographic Analysis" (DA)[45] that was used to evaluate coverage and estimate net undercount[46] in the 1940 through 2000 censuses. DA uses administrative records, including birth and death records, together with estimates of net international migration to the United States during a decade, to estimate the population size at a given census date. This figure is compared with the population count from the actual census to arrive at estimates of coverage and net undercount. The Bureau has described the process as follows:

The traditional DA population benchmarks are developed for the census date by analyzing various types of demographic data essentially independent of the census, such as administrative statistics on births, deaths, authorized international migration, and Medicare enrollments, as well as estimates of legal emigration and net unauthorized immigration. The difference between the Demographic Analysis benchmarks and the census count provides an estimate of the census net undercount. Dividing the net undercount by the DA benchmark[s] provides an estimate of the net undercount rate.[47]

Despite its utility, demographic analysis has limitations. Among them are the feasibility of producing estimates only at the national level, not at lower geographic levels, and only for broad racial categories (Black and non-Black).[48] Uncertainty in estimating the components of net international migration to the United States, particularly emigration, temporary migration, and unauthorized migration, is another concern with DA.[49] According to the Bureau, "the research effect on immigration, births, and deaths led to Revised DA estimates" for 1990 and 2000. "The Revised DA lowered the estimated net undercount rates from 1.85% to 1.65% in 1990, and from 0.32% to 0.12% in 2000, but did not alter the DA finding that the estimated net undercount rate in 2000 was substantially lower than in 1990."[50]

Table 2 shows net percentage undercount estimates for the past seven censuses, as derived by demographic analysis. The last two columns of the table, for 1990 and 2000, reflect the revised DA estimates discussed above. The table indicates a decrease in the estimated net undercount rates for the total population, Blacks, and non-Blacks in every census year except 1990, when the rates increased for the overall population and the two groups within it. In each of the seven censuses, the differential undercount persisted: the estimated net rate was higher for Blacks than for non-Blacks.

On December 6, 2010, the Bureau released DA estimates of the population as of Census Day. They were presented in five series, ranging from low to high. Although the estimates ultimately may serve to indicate 2010 census quality, the Bureau will not use demographic analysis to estimate net undercount. The Bureau attributed the change from past decades to the uncertainties inherent in constructing DA estimates.[51]

Table 2. Percentage Net Decennial Census Undercount by Race, as Estimated by Demographic Analysis, 1940 through 2000

	1940	1950	1960	1970	1980	1990	2000
Total population	5.4%	4.1%	3.1%	2.7%	1.2%	1.65%	0.12%
Black	8.4%	7.5%	6.6%	6.5%	4.5%	5.52%	2.78%
Non-Black	5.0%	3.8%	2.7%	2.2%	0.8%	1.08%	-0.29%

Sources: Estimates for 1940 through1980 are from J.G. Robinson, et al., "Estimates of Population Coverage in the 1990 United States Census Based on Demographic Analysis," *Journal of the American Statistical Association*, vol. 88 (September 1993), p. 1065, reprinted in U.S. Bureau of the Census, *Accuracy and Coverage Evaluation, Statement on the Feasibility of Using Statistical Methods to Improve the Accuracy of Census 2000*, June 2000 (unpublished document). Estimates for 1990 and 2000 are from U.S. Bureau of the Census, *Coverage Measurement from the Perspective of March 2001 Accuracy and Coverage Evaluation*, Census 2000 Topic Report no. 4 (Washington: U.S. Bureau of the Census, February 2004), p. 9.

Note: All numbers except one indicate net percentage undercounts of the total population or groups within the population. The exception, -0.29% for non-Blacks in 2000, indicates a net overcount of this group.

Survey Estimates of Census Coverage

To evaluate coverage in the three most recent enumerations, the Bureau used not only demographic analysis, but other means as well: in 1980, the Post Enumeration Program; in 1990, the Post Enumeration Survey; and in 2000, Accuracy and Coverage Evaluation. Each evaluation involved taking a post-census survey, designed to be statistically independent of the census, and comparing the survey with the census results to estimate omissions from the census and erroneous enumerations. These surveys were, as all are, subject to sampling and other errors.

- The 1980 census Post Enumeration Program yielded informative studies of the estimation methods and results, rather than specific coverage estimates.[52]
- The 1990 census Post Enumeration Survey estimates indicated a net percentage undercount of 1.61% for the total population, 0.68% for non-Hispanic Whites, 4.57% for Blacks, 2.36% for Asians or Pacific

Islanders, 12.22% for American Indians on reservations, and 4.99% for Hispanics.[53]

- The presentation of data by race and ethnicity changed somewhat between the 1990 and 2000 censuses, making certain categories (for example, Blacks in 1990 versus non-Hispanic Blacks in 2000) not perfectly comparable. The final 2000 census Accuracy and Coverage Evaluation estimates indicated a net percentage overcount of -0.49% for the total population, -1.13% for non-Hispanic Whites, - 0.75% for non-Hispanic Asians, and -0.88% for American Indians on reservations (with each minus sign signifying an overcount). The estimated net percentage undercount for non-Hispanic Blacks was 1.84%; for native Hawaiians or other Pacific Islanders, 2.12%; for American Indians off reservations, 0.62%; and for Hispanics, 0.71%.[54]

Reporting in April 2010 on the status of the Bureau's coverage evaluation for the current census, the Census Coverage Measurement (CCM) program, GAO explained that

> The Bureau has developed separate address lists—one for the entire nation of over 134 million housing units that it will use to conduct the census and one for coverage measurement sample areas—and will collect each set of data through independent operations. For the 2010 Census, census operations began collecting population data from households in January 2010 and will continue through the end of July, while CCM operations will collect data by visiting each of the housing units in the coverage measurement sample during an operation called Person Interviewing from August through October.[55]
>
> The statistical methodology the Bureau uses to estimate net coverage errors relies on an assumption that the chance that a person is counted by the census is not affected by whether he or she is counted in the independent coverage measurement sample, or vice versa. Because violating this "independence" assumption can bias coverage estimates, the Bureau takes special measures to maintain CCM's separation from the census, such as developing a separate address list for the coverage measurement sample....[56]

GAO noted that in December 2009 the Bureau Director approved several changes in CCM, including higher "reinterview rates for CCM field work to improve quality assurance"; additional training of workers for person interviewing, to help them deal with "special situations due to current economic conditions," such as increased homelessness; higher "supervisor-to-employee field staffing ratios to improve quality ... of field work"; and a new "telephone-based study" of "how well respondents recall information about their residence and possible movement since Census Day."[57] To offset the expense of these extra measures, the Bureau authorized an almost 45% reduction in CCM sample size.[58] The cut, in GAO's assessment, would "reduce precision of the estimates, yet the proposed changes should reduce nonsampling errors and thus provide users with more reliable estimates."[59] Perhaps because of what the 2010 census is already likely to cost, the option of making changes to improve CCM data quality without decreasing sample size was not addressed.

The report critiqued certain aspects of the CCM program. One observation was that even though the Bureau had "stated the importance of using 2010 evaluation data ... for 2020 Census design," it had "not yet taken steps to link CCM data" to improvements for 2020.[60] Another point, particularly relevant for future census evaluations, was that the Bureau should ascertain the "optimal time" to start person interviewing for CCM. If this operation begins too early, it can overlap "with census data collection, possibly compromising the independence of the two different operations and introducing a 'contamination bias' error into CCM data." Starting person interviewing too late "increases the chance that respondents will not accurately remember household information from Census Day ... introducing error (known as 'recall bias') in the CCM count." Either error "could affect the Bureau's conclusions about the accuracy of the census."[61]

The Bureau announced on November 1, 2010, that it had completed all CCM interviews. The results of the program will not be available until 2012, however.[62]

Coverage Evaluation Surveys and the Census Adjustment Issue

Although conducting surveys to evaluate census coverage is an established practice, the survey results never have been used to correct or "adjust" miscounts in the decennial numbers that constitute the official state population counts for House apportionment. The Supreme Court ruled in 1999 (525 U.S. 316 (1999)) that adjustment of the apportionment numbers would be illegal under Title 13 U.S.C., Section 195, but was silent about whether it would be unconstitutional. The issue was contentious for at least two decades before the 1999 Court ruling and, despite it, continues to generate controversy.

Whereas supporters of adjustment argue that it is necessary to rectify the undercount problem, opponents maintain that use of the procedure would make the census vulnerable to political manipulation.

Then-Acting Bureau Director Thomas Mesenbourg, when asked by the ranking member of the House Subcommittee on Information Policy, Census, and National Archives at a March 5, 2009, census oversight hearing if the Bureau would conduct a census coverage evaluation survey in 2010, replied that it would.[63] "The focus of the 2010 coverage measurement program," he explained, would be "to provide better information about the components of error. So we'll be providing data not only on the net error, but also components of error such as duplicates, omissions, and so on."[64] Responding to a question about whether the Bureau intended to use the program for adjustment, Mesenbourg said that it did not.[65]

Nevertheless, the Obama Administration's nominations of Gary Locke, the former Governor of Washington, to be Commerce Secretary and Robert M. Groves, a survey research expert and demographer, as Census Bureau Director provided occasions for some Members of Congress to seek further assurance that sampling for adjustment would not play a role in the 2010 census.

Locke told the Senate Committee on Commerce, Science, and Transportation at his March 18, 2009, confirmation hearing, "The Supreme Court has made it very clear that statistical sampling is not permissible for apportionment purposes. That is the law. We will enforce the law."[66] The committee's ranking member then noted that "the Supreme Court did not specifically mention ... intrastate redistricting" and asked whether sampling would be used to adjust the data for this purpose.[67] The nominee replied, "It is my understanding that there are no plans in the Department of Commerce or the Census Bureau to use any type of statistical sampling with respect to [the] population count."[68] On March 24, 2009, the Senate confirmed Locke's nomination.[69]

The Senate approved Groves's nomination on July 13, 2009.[70] The new Director previously headed the University of Michigan's Survey Research Center. From 1990 to 1992, he was an Associate Director of the Census Bureau,[71] where, according to press reports, he differed with George H. W. Bush Administration officials over his support for 1990 census adjustment.[72]

Groves's written opening remarks at his May 15, 2009, confirmation hearing before the Senate Committee on Homeland Security and Governmental Affairs stated, however, "I agree fully with Secretary Locke's testimony that statistical adjustment of the census is eliminated as an option for apportionment and further that statistical adjustment will not be used for redistricting. The 2003 decision of [then-Census Bureau] director Kincannon, consistent with this, assured that no implementation infrastructure for adjustment was put in place for 2010."[73]

The committee's ranking member observed that although sampling could not be used to adjust the census apportionment numbers, "There is ... some question over whether sampling could be used for redistricting and for the allocation of federal funds." She then asked Groves, "Will you advocate for the statistical adjustment or use of sampling during the 2010 Census?" He answered, "No, Senator," and added in response to the same query about the 2020 census, "I have no plans to do that for 2020."[74]

In April 2010, as previously discussed, GAO issued its observations to date about the 2010 Census Coverage Measurement program. The report, requested by the ranking members of the House Oversight and Government Reform Committee and the Information Policy, Census, and National Archives Subcommittee, repeated others' earlier assurances that the "Bureau is not planning to use CCM to adjust the 2010 Census. Instead, CCM will be used to evaluate coverage error to improve the 2020 and future censuses."[75]

EFFORTS TOWARD AN EQUITABLE CENSUS

Communications Outreach

Because census accuracy and coverage are likely to persist as issues after the decennial count, the Bureau addressed the need to publicize the census, then convince as many people as possible to complete and return their 2010 census questionnaires, or to respond if contacted by an enumerator. The various components of the Bureau's integrated communications strategy were designed to meet this two-part goal. As GAO observed, however, motivating the public to respond to the census was "a far thornier task" than raising awareness about it.[76]

On September 6, 2007, the Bureau announced that it had awarded the 2010 census communications contract to Draftfcb of New York City. Draftfcb headed a team of communications firms that specialize in reaching minority groups: Global Hue, for Blacks and Hispanics; IW Group, for Asians, Native Hawaiians, and other Pacific Islanders; G&G, for American Indians and Alaska Natives; and Allied Media, for "emerging" groups, such as Arabic-speaking people and Eastern Europeans.[77] The integrated communications strategy was built on the partnership and Census in Schools programs, as well as on paid advertising via network and cable television, radio, the Internet, newspapers, and magazines.[78]

For the 2010 census, as for that in 2000, the Bureau partnered with local governments, businesses, community organizations, neighborhood groups, and the media to help inform the public about the census and encourage participation in it, including cooperation with enumerators during nonresponse follow-up. The Bureau's website presented partnership information, for example, a list of partners.[79]

Among the activities the Bureau suggested for local governments, businesses, organizations, and groups were distributing census promotional materials, sponsoring events to raise awareness of the census, and disseminating information about it through newsletters. Partnership staff, working with elected officials, formed Complete Count Committees to reach traditionally undercounted groups. Early in 2009, the Bureau mailed Complete Count Committee guides to the highest elected officials in 39,000 state, local, and tribal governments.[80]

Partners also could identify possible candidates for temporary census work, such as enumerators to conduct NRFU, and provide space for testing job applicants and training new hires. The Bureau's website gave information about 2010 census employment.[81] As of April 11, 2010, the Bureau had slightly exceeded its goal of recruiting 3.7 million applicants for more than 600,000 census-taker and other positions related to NRFU.[82] The weak economy may have given the Bureau a recruitment advantage, even for short-term, often part-time, jobs.

The Bureau invited local-government partners to participate, as they did for the 2000 census, in the Local Update of Census Addresses (LUCA) campaign. LUCA was made possible by P.L. 103- 430 (108 Stat. 4394) to assist the Bureau in improving the Master Address File. Under the program, local, state, and tribal governments could review MAF and document any mistakes they found in it. LUCA for the 2010 census began in January 2007. According to the Bureau, it received the LUCA data and entered them into MAF.[83] LUCA participants could review the changes made and appeal requested changes that were not accepted.[84]

The Census in Schools initiative for 2010 focused on educating children in kindergarten through 12th grade about the importance of census participation, so that they could convey this message to their parents.[85] Scholastic, Inc., joined with the Bureau to produce English and Spanish teaching guides, lesson plans, maps, brochures, and take-home materials for students, all of which were posted on the Census-in-Schools website[86] and on Scholastic.com. Printed materials were distributed to public and private schools nationwide.[87]

Questionnaire Outreach

The conventional mail-out of 2010 census questionnaires to about 120 million U.S. households was discussed earlier in this report. Noted below are other operations, which focused on the hardto-count.

Approximately 13 million bilingual census forms, in English and Spanish, were mailed to neighborhoods with high concentrations of Spanish-speaking residents.[88] Questionnaires in Spanish, Chinese, Korean, Vietnamese, and Russian, along with guides in 59 languages other than English, were made available upon request.[89] In addition, for people who did not receive census forms at their homes, "Be Counted" forms in English and the five other languages listed above were placed in various public locations, such as libraries, community centers, and places of worship. The Bureau also provided telephone assistance, including assistance for the hearing impaired, as well as Braille and large-print questionnaire guides.[90]

In March and April 2010, the Bureau undertook the enumeration of residents in what GAO has termed "diverse dwellings," including migrant-worker housing, boats, college dormitories, nursing homes, and prisons.[91] Service-based enumeration, which took place at the end of March, was designed to count the homeless at places where they receive assistance, such as soup kitchens and mobile food vans. A count of people living outdoors occurred at the same time.[92]

The Bureau also implemented procedures whereby address listers, during address canvassing, could identify possibly inhabitable housing units in areas of Louisiana, Mississippi, and Texas that were damaged by Gulf Coast hurricanes Katrina and Rita in 2005 and Ike in 2008. Then, in a March 2010 update-leave operation, field workers hand delivered about 1.2 million census forms to these units, some of which were not on the Bureau's address list. Besides leaving questionnaires to be completed and returned by mail, the workers made any necessary updates to addresses and maps.[93]

Update leave was used as well in places throughout the United States "where the 'address' may not reflect the actual location of the housing unit," and in areas "that do not receive either regular or at-home mail delivery."[94] About 12 million questionnaires were hand delivered, including the previously mentioned 1.2 million in certain Gulf Coast areas.

Protecting Data Confidentiality and Quality, Public Safety, and Census Objectivity

The Census Bureau is staffed by federal career civilians, many of whom are trained as statisticians, demographers, and IT professionals. Title 13 U.S.C. provides for a series of penalties against any Bureau officer or employee found to have committed certain offenses. These penalties have been adjusted in accordance with provisions of the Sentencing Reform Act of 1984, Title 18 U.S.C., Sections 3559 and 3571. Whoever neglects or refuses to perform his or her duties (Title 13, Section 212) can be fined not more than $5,000. A Bureau officer or employee can be fined not more than $250,000 or imprisoned not more than five years, or both, if the person "willfully and knowingly swears or affirms falsely as to the truth of any statement required" of him or her; "willfully and knowingly makes a false certificate or fictitious return"; or "knowingly or willfully" supplies or supplied "any false statement or false information with reference to any inquiry" for which the person "was authorized and required to collect information" (Title 13, Section 213). Wrongful disclosure of confidential information (Title 13, Section 214) can result in a fine of not more than $250,000 or not more than five years' imprisonment, or both.

Besides operating under these constraints, 2010 census workers were subject to Federal Bureau of Investigation (FBI) background checks of their names and fingerprints, at an estimated cost of $450 million for fingerprinting.[95] According to March 2010 congressional testimony by GAO, about 22% of those hired for address canvassing had unclassifiable prints, generally due to local census office workers' errors in taking the prints for submission to the FBI.[96] The Census Bureau tried to obtain clearer prints of nonresponse follow-up hires through improved training of the local census office workers and by supplying each office with at least one digital fingerprint scanner. The Bureau estimated that about 10% to 12% of workers, instead of 22%, would have unclassifiable prints when the scanners were used.[97] If, as GAO testified, the fingerprint check during address canvassing revealed "a criminal record that made an employee unsuitable for employment, the Bureau either terminated the person immediately or placed the individual in a nonworking status until the matter was resolved."[98] Address-canvassing hires whose prints were unclassifiable "were allowed to continue working if their name background check was acceptable." GAO "did not receive a response from the Bureau" about whether it would "allow ... workers with unclassifiable prints to continue" NRFU work.[99] Congress could choose to review the problems encountered in the fingerprinting operation, their implications for public safety, the delayed decision to use digital scanners, and the operation's final cost.

The Bureau Director, in contrast to other Bureau officers and employees, is a presidential appointee. News articles,[100] early in the Obama Administration, stating that the Director might report to the White House, instead of, as Title 13 U.S.C. stipulates, the Commerce Secretary, [101] raised concern among some Members of Congress that the 2010 count could be subject to political manipulation. Subsequent articles[102] about Administration assurances that the Director would continue reporting to the Secretary did not entirely allay this concern. Gary Locke, speaking to the Senate Commerce, Science, and Transportation Committee on March 18, 2009, before his confirmation as Commerce Secretary, emphasized that the decennial census "will be run out of the Department of Commerce and by a Director who will work with the Congress, the Administration, and our state and local leaders ... in making this a successful count."[103] Robert M. Groves's written opening remarks to the Senate Homeland Security and Governmental Affairs Committee at the May 15, 2009, hearing on his nomination to be Bureau Director stated that "government statistical agencies must be independent of partisan politics" and that "this country needs an objective, nonpartisan, professional Census Bureau."[104]

The Bureau, in all matters related to the decennial enumeration and the rest of its activities under Title 13 U.S.C., is subject to oversight. In the 111th Congress, the House Oversight and Government Reform Committee, Information Policy, Census, and National Archives Subcommittee, and the Senate Homeland Security and Governmental Affairs Committee, Federal Financial Management, Government Information, Federal Services, and International Security Subcommittee, conducted decennial census oversight hearings. A change in the 112th Congress is that the House Oversight and Government Reform Committee's Health Care, District of Columbia, Census, and National Archives Subcommittee has Census Bureau oversight. The Bureau's operations and funding requests receive further attention from the House and Senate Appropriations Committees. The relevant Appropriations Subcommittees in the 112th Congress are those on Commerce, Justice, Science, and Related Agencies. The Government Accountability Office also has evaluated various aspects of the 2010 census and has issued many reports, some of which this CRS report has cited. In addition, the MITRE Corporation advised the Bureau periodically about its IT programs for the 2010 census and, as previously mentioned, noted serious problems with the plans the Bureau once had for Field Data Collection Automation.[105] The National Academy of Sciences' Committee on National Statistics (CNSTAT), established in 1972 "to provide an independent and objective resource for evaluating and improving the work of the highly decentralized U.S. federal statistical system,"[106] evaluated the 2010 census research program, especially in relation to 2020 census planning.[107]

A decade ago, the bipartisan Census Monitoring Board, established under Section 210 of P.L. 105-119 (111 Stat. 2440), scrutinized the objectivity of the 2000 census. Section 210 provided for an eight-member board, with two members appointed by the Senate majority leader; two by the Speaker of the House; and four by the President, one at the recommendation of the Senate minority leader and one as recommended by the House minority leader.

The function of the board was "to observe and monitor all aspects of the preparation and implementation of the 2000 decennial census." Each co-chairman of the board, along with any staff designated by the co-chairs, was to have "access to any data, files, information, or other matters maintained by the Bureau of the Census (or received by it in the course of conducting a decennial census of population) which they may request."

The board was to prepare interim and final reports for Congress. The final report, due by September 1, 2001,[108] was to "contain a detailed statement of the findings and conclusions of the Board." All reports were to address, among other matters, the degree to which the Census Bureau's preparations for Census 2000 "shall achieve maximum possible accuracy at every level of geography"; "shall be taken by means of an enumeration process designed to count every individual possible"; and "shall be free from political bias and arbitrary decisions."

The law authorized $4 million in appropriations for the board in each fiscal year from FY1998 through FY2001. The board went out of existence on September 30, 2001.

CONCLUDING OBSERVATIONS

The Census Bureau's mandate to conduct the 2010 decennial census, which would have been demanding and costly under the best circumstances, faced additional challenges because the Bureau's contract with the Harris Corporation to produce handheld computers for Field Data Collection Automation yielded only partial success. The Bureau's decision not to use the handhelds for nonresponse follow-up called into question whether a paper-based NRFU, with persistent IT problems, could account adequately for historically under-enumerated population groups. The Bureau reported an encouraging national participation rate of 74% for the mail-out, mail-back part of the census, but it has yet to estimate, through the Census Coverage Measurement program, how well the census accounted for the whole population. Although the Bureau has completed interviewing for the CCM survey, the CCM findings will not be available until 2012. Concerns about possible bias in the enumeration, and about whom the census counts, miscounts, or omits, likely will persist into the future because the census numbers serve such important national, state, and local purposes.

End Notes

[1] U.S. Bureau of the Census, "How It Benefits Your Community,"http://2010.census.gov/2010census/ about/community-benefits.php; and testimony of then-Acting Census Bureau Director Thomas Mesenbourg in U.S. Congress, House Committee on Oversight and Government Reform, Subcommittee on Information Policy, Census, and National Archives, *Census Data and Their Use in Federal Formula Funding*, 111th Cong., 1st sess., July 9, 2009 (Washington: 2009), p. 2.

[2] U.S. Bureau of the Census, "Methodology for the United States Resident Population Estimates by Age, Sex, Race, and Hispanic Origin (Vintage 2008): April 1, 2000 to July 1, 2008," http://www.census.gov/popest/topics/ methodology/2008-nat-meth.html; and U.S. Bureau of the Census, "2008 National Population Projections Methodology Summary Document" and "Methodology Summary for the Interim Population Projections for States by Age and Sex: 2004-2030," http://www.census.gov/population/www/projections/methodology.html.

[3] See, for example, the testimony of then-Census Bureau Director Steve Murdock in U.S. Congress, House Committee on Appropriations, Subcommittee on Commerce, Justice, Science, and Related Agencies, *The Fiscal Year 2009 Budget*, hearing, 110th Cong., 2nd sess., April 3, 2008 (Washington: 2008), p. 4.

[4] Testimony of Associate Census Bureau Director Arnold Jackson in U.S. Congress, House Committee on Oversight and Government Reform, Subcommittee on Information Policy, Census, and National Archives, *2010 Census: A Status Update of Key Decennial Operations*, March 25, 2010, pp. 2-3, http://www.census.gov/newsroom/releases/pdf/ AAJ_Testimony_3-25-10.pdf.

[5] U.S. Government Accountability Office, *2010 Census: Cooperation with Enumerators Is Critical to a Successful Headcount*, GAO-10-665T, April 30, 2010, p. 3.

[6] U.S. Bureau of the Census, "Nation Achieves 74 Percent Final Mail Participation in 2010 Census," press release CB10-CN.81, October 21, 2010, p. 1. This percentage matched the 2000 census mail participation rate. The Bureau termed this rate a "fairer measure" of census compliance than the "mail response rate." The reason is that the denominator for the participation rate excludes housing units from which the U.S. Postal Service returned forms as "undeliverable" (an indication that these units were vacant), but the response rate includes these units in the denominator. U.S. Bureau of the Census, "2010 Census Participation Rates," http://2010.census.gov/2010census/ take10map/. The national mail

response rate as of April 19, 2010, was 63.2%; the Bureau had predicted that it would be between 59% and 65%. U.S. Government Accountability Office, *2010 Census: Cooperation with Enumerators Is Critical to a Successful Headcount*, GAO-10-665T, April 30, 2010, highlights page.

[7] U.S. Bureau of the Census, "$1.6 Billion in 2010 Census Savings Returned," press release CB10-CN.70, August 10, 2010, p. 1.

[8] U.S. Bureau of the Census, "Nation Achieves 74 Percent Final Mail Participation in 2010 Census," press release CB10-CN.81, October 21, 2010, p. 1.

[9] U.S. Bureau of the Census, "U.S. Census Bureau Announces 2010 Census Population Counts— Apportionment Counts Delivered to President," press release CB10-CN.93, December 21, 2010.

[10] The Bureau's earlier use of sampling was not in the decennial census, but in a 1937 survey to gauge the extent of unemployment in the nation during the Great Depression. U.S. Bureau of the Census, "History: 1930 Overview," http://www.census.gov/history/www/through _the_decades/overview/1930.html, and "History: 1940 (Population)," http://www.census. gov/history/www/through _the _decades/index_of_questions/ 1940_population.html.

[11] U.S. Bureau of the Census, "History: 1970 (Population)," http://www.census. gov/history/www/through_the_ decades/ index_of_questions/1970_population.html.

[12] U.S. Bureau of the Census, *Measuring America: The Decennial Censuses from 1790 to 2000* (Washington: GPO, 2002), p. 98.

[13] U.S. Bureau of the Census, "Explore the Form," http://2010.census.gov/ 2010census/about/interactive-form.php. The short form asked certain additional questions for administrative purposes, such as the number of people living in the housing unit on April 1, 2010, their names, and the telephone number of the person completing the form. The Bureau collected this information "to ensure response accuracy and completeness and to contact respondents whose forms have incomplete or missing information." Ibid.

[14] U.S. Bureau of the Census, *American Community Survey, Design and Methodology* (Washington: GPO, 2009), p. 2-1.

[15] U.S. Bureau of the Census, "Quick Guide to the American Community Survey (ACS) Products in American FactFinder," pp. 1, 3, http://factfinder.census.gov/home/saff/aff_acs2009 _quickguide.pdf.

[16] U.S. Bureau of the Census, *United States Census 2010, High Risk Improvement Plan*, version 7-2, November 4, 2008, p. 2.

[17] U.S. Government Accountability Office, *Information Technology: Census Bureau Testing of 2010 Decennial Systems Can Be Strengthened*, GAO-09-262, March 2009.

[18] Testimony of then-Census Bureau Director Steve Murdock in U.S. Congress, House Committee on Appropriations, Subcommittee on Commerce, Justice, Science, and Related Agencies, *The Fiscal Year 2009 Budget*, hearing, 110th Cong., 2nd sess., April 3, 2008 (Washington: 2008).

[19] U.S. Department of Commerce, Office of Inspector General, *Top Management Challenges Facing the Department of Commerce*, Final Report no. OIG-19384 (Washington: U.S. Department of Commerce, 2008), p. 1.

[20] U.S. Government Accountability Office, *2010 Census: Plans for Decennial Census Operations and Technology Have Progressed, but Much Uncertainty Remains*, GAO-08-886T, June 11, 2008, p. 1.

[21] U.S. Congress, House Committee on Appropriations, *Commerce, Justice, Science, and Related Agencies Appropriations Bill, 2010*, report to accompany H.R. 2847, 111th Cong., 1st sess., H.Rept. 111-149 (Washington: GPO, 2009), p. 18. For information about the Bureau's

FY2010 appropriations, see CRS Report R40644, *Commerce, Justice, Science, and Related Agencies: FY2010 Appropriations*, coordinated by Nathan James, Oscar R. Gonzales, and Jennifer D. Williams. See also CRS Report R41161, *Commerce, Justice, Science, and Related Agencies: FY2011 Appropriations*, coordinated by Nathan James, Oscar R. Gonzales, and Jennifer D. Williams.

[22] U.S. Government Accountability Office, *2010 Census: Cooperation with Enumerators Is Critical to a Successful Headcount*, GAO-10-665T, April 30, 2010, p. 3. The actual cost of the 2010 census cannot be known for some time. Shortly after NRFU ended, however, the Bureau reported that it had not had to use $1.6 billion of the funds available for the 2010 census. The Bureau attributed the savings to the relatively high 74% mail response rate, which meant less nonresponse follow-up; to the greater productivity of NRFU workers in 2010 than in 2000; and to the absence of "disasters or major operational breakdowns" that would have necessitated drawing on contingency funds. U.S. Bureau of the Census, "$1.6 Billion in 2010 Census Savings Returned," press release CB10-CN.70, August 10, 2010, p. 1.

[23] U.S. Department of Commerce, Office of Inspector General, *Top Management Challenges Facing the Department of Commerce*, Final Report no. OIG-19384 (Washington: U.S. Department of Commerce, 2008), p. 2.

[24] Ibid.

[25] Ibid., pp. 3-4. The MITRE quotation appeared earlier in Allan Holmes, "Census program to use handheld computers said to be in 'serious trouble'," GovernmentExecutive.com, January 2, 2008, http://www.govexec.com/story_page.cfm? filepath=/dailyfed/0108/010208h1.htm. This article contained a link to the source of the quotation, MITRE's November 29, 2007, "Talking Points for Meeting with [then-Census Bureau Deputy Director] Jay Waite."

[26] U.S. Department of Commerce, Office of Inspector General, *Top Management Challenges Facing the Department of Commerce*, Final Report no. OIG-19384 (Washington: U.S. Department of Commerce, 2008), p. 2.

[27] See, for example, U.S. Government Accountability Office, *Information Technology: Census Bureau Needs to Improve Its Risk Management of Decennial Systems*, GAO-08-79, October 5, 2007.

[28] U.S. Government Accountability Office, Office of the Comptroller General, "GAO Lists Top 'Urgent Issues' for Next President and Congress; Unveils New Transition Web Site," press release, November 6, 2008, p. 1.

[29] U.S. Government Accountability Office, *High-Risk Series: An Update*, GAO-09-271, January 22, 2009.

[30] GAO wrote that the Dress Rehearsal period spanned February 2006 through June 2009. During it, the Bureau developed and tested "systems and operations, and it held a mock Census Day on May 1, 2008." U.S. Government Accountability Office, *Information Technology: Census Bureau Testing of 2010 Decennial Systems Can Be Strengthened*, GAO-09-262, March 2009, p. 9. Beyond the Dress Rehearsal tests, the Bureau did "supplementary testing to prepare for the 2010 Decennial Census." Ibid., p. 10.

[31] Group quarters, the addresses of which had to be validated, cover a wide variety of group housing, including college residence halls, military barracks, nursing homes, and prisons. U.S. Government Accountability Office, *Information Technology: Census Bureau Testing of 2010 Decennial Systems Can Be Strengthened*, GAO-09-262, March 2009, p. 3.

[32] Ibid., pp. 21-22.

[33] Ibid., p. 28.

[34] Ibid., p. 17.
[35] Ibid., p. 4.
[36] Testimony of Commerce Department Associate Deputy Inspector General Judith Gordon in U.S. Congress, House Committee on Oversight and Government Reform, Subcommittee on Information Policy, Census, and National Archives, *The 2010 Census: An Assessment of the Bureau's Preparedness*, March 25, 2010 (Washington: 2010), p. 2.
[37] Ibid.
[38] U.S. Government Accountability Office, *2010 Census: Data Collection Is Under Way, but Reliability of Key Information Technology Systems Remains a Risk*, GAO-10-567T, March 25, 2010, p. 3.
[39] Ibid., pp. 7-8.
[40] Ibid., p. 8.
[41] Ibid., pp. 8-9.
[42] U.S. Government Accountability Office, *2010 Census: Cooperation with Enumerators Is Critical to a Successful Headcount*, GAO-10-665T, April 30, 2010, p. 8.
[43] U.S. Government Accountability Office, *2010 Census: Data Collection Operations Were Generally Completed as Planned, but Long-standing Challenges Suggest Need for Fundamental Reforms*, GAO-11-193, p. 20.
[44] Ibid., p. 21.
[45] U.S. Bureau of the Census, *Accuracy and Coverage Evaluation, Statement on the Feasibility of Using Statistical Methods to Improve the Accuracy of Census 2000*, June 2000 (unpublished document), p. 4.
[46] "The difference between the true, but unknown, population count and an original census count is called the net undercount." Kirk M. Wolter, "Accounting for America's Uncounted and Miscounted," *Science*, vol. 253 (July 1991), p. 12.
[47] U.S. Bureau of the Census, *Coverage Measurement from the Perspective of March 2001 Accuracy and Coverage Evaluation*, Census 2000 Topic Report no. 4 (Washington: U.S. Bureau of the Census, February 2004), p. 7.
[48] Ibid., p. 9.
[49] Ibid., p. 7.
[50] Ibid.
[51] U.S. Bureau of the Census, "U.S. Census Bureau Releases 2010 Demographic Analysis Population Estimates," CB10-CN.87, December 6, 2010.
[52] U.S. Bureau of the Census, *Accuracy and Coverage Evaluation, Statement on the Feasibility of Using Statistical Methods to Improve the Accuracy of Census 2000*, June 2000 (unpublished document), p. 20.
[53] U.S. Bureau of the Census, *A.C.E. Revision II, Summary of Estimated Net Coverage*, Memorandum Series PP-54, December 31, 2002, p. 3, http://www.census.gov/dmd/www/ace2.html.
[54] Ibid.
[55] U.S. Government Accountability Office, *2010 Census: Plans for Census Coverage Measurement Are on Track, but Additional Steps Will Improve Its Usefulness*, GAO-10-324, April 2010, p. 4.
[56] Ibid.
[57] Ibid., p. 6.
[58] Ibid. A year earlier, the Bureau had estimated that the sample size would be about 300,000 housing units, the same as in the 2000 census Accuracy and Coverage Evaluation. See testimony of then-Acting Census Bureau Director Thomas Mesenbourg in U.S. Congress,

House Committee on Oversight and Government Reform, Subcommittee on Information Policy, Census, and National Archives, *Critical Operations of the 2010 Census—Status Update*, hearing, 111th Cong., 1st sess., March 5, 2009 (Washington: 2009).

[59] U.S. Government Accountability Office, *2010 Census: Plans for Census Coverage Measurement Are on Track, but Additional Steps Will Improve Its Usefulness*, GAO-10-324, April 2010, p. 6.

[60] Ibid., p. 10.

[61] Ibid., p. 8.

[62] U.S. Bureau of the Census, "Operational Press Briefing," transcript, November 1, 2010, pp. 2, 14.

[63] Testimony of then-Acting Census Bureau Director Thomas Mesenbourg in U.S. Congress, House Committee on Oversight and Government Reform, Subcommittee on Information Policy, Census, and National Archives, *Critical Operations of the 2010 Census—Status Update*, hearing, 111th Cong., 1st sess., March 5, 2009 (Washington: 2009).

[64] Ibid.

[65] Ibid.

[66] U.S. Congress, Senate Committee on Commerce, Science, and Transportation, "Senator Hutchison Presses Commerce Nominee Locke to Ensure a Fair and Open Census Process," press release, March 18, 2009, p. 2.

[67] Ibid.

[68] Ibid.

[69] "Department of Commerce, Gary Locke, of Washington, to Be Secretary of Commerce," *Congressional Record*, daily edition, vol. 155 (March 24, 2009), p. S3734.

[70] "Nomination of Robert M. Groves to Be Director of the Census," *Congressional Record*, daily edition, vol. 155 (July 13, 2009), p. S7402.

[71] The White House, Office of the Press Secretary, "President Obama Announces More Key Administration Posts," press release, April 2, 2009.

[72] See Carrie Dann, "Census Nomination Renews 'Statistical Adjustment' Debate," *Congress Daily AM*, NationalJournal.com, April 3, 2009, copy available from the CRS author; Randy James, "Robert M. Groves: Obama's Pick for Census Chief," Time.com, April 7, 2009, http://www.time.com/time/nation/article/0,8599,1889793,00.html; and "Obama Taps Robert Groves to Be Census Director," Fox News.com, April 2, 2009, http://www.foxnews.com/politics/first100days/2009/04/02/obama-taps-robert-groves-census-director/.

[73] Testimony of Robert M. Groves in U.S. Congress, Senate Committee on Homeland Security and Governmental Affairs, *Nomination of Robert M. Groves to Be Director of the Census*, hearing, 111th Cong., 1st sess., May 15, 2009 (Washington: 2009). For the full text of his opening remarks, see http://hsgac.senate.gov/public/_files/ 051509Groves.pdf.

[74] Questions by Sen. Susan M. Collins in U.S. Congress, Senate Committee on Homeland Security and Governmental Affairs, *Nomination of Robert M. Groves to Be Director of the Census*, hearing, 111th Cong., 1st sess., May 15, 2009 (Washington: 2009).

[75] U.S. Government Accountability Office, *2010 Census: Plans for Census Coverage Measurement Are on Track, but Additional Steps Will Improve Its Usefulness*, GAO-10-324, April 2010, p. 3.

[76] U.S. Government Accountability Office, *2010 Census: Communications Campaign Has Potential to Boost Participation*, GAO-09-525T, March 23, 2009, p. 2.

[77] U.S. Bureau of the Census, "Census Bureau Announces Award of 2010 Census Communications Contract," press release, September 7, 2007.

[78] U.S. Bureau of the Census, *2010 Census Integrated Communications Campaign Synopsis*, March 2009, http://2010.census.gov/partners/pdf/Census_Plan_Synopsis_5-9-09.pdf.

[79] U.S. Bureau of the Census, "Our Partners," http://2010.census.gov/partners/.

[80] Testimony of then-Acting Census Bureau Director Thomas Mesenbourg in U.S. Congress, House Committee on Oversight and Government Reform, Subcommittee on Information Policy, Census, and National Archives, *Census 2010: Assessing the Bureau's Strategies for Reducing the Undercount of Hard-to-Count Populations*, hearing, 111th Cong., 1st sess., March 23, 2009 (Washington: 2009), p. 5.

[81] U.S. Bureau of the Census, "2010 Census Jobs," http://2010.census.gov/2010censusjobs/.

[82] U.S. Government Accountability Office, *2010 Census: Cooperation with Enumerators Is Critical to a Successful Headcount*, GAO-10-665T, April 30, 2010, p. 6.

[83] Information obtained at a December 18, 2008, meeting between the CRS author and officials from the Census Bureau's Decennial Management Division, Office of the Associate Director for Communications, and Congressional Affairs Office.

[84] U.S. Bureau of the Census, "2010 Decennial Census Local Update of Census Addresses (LUCA)," http://www.census.gov/geo/www/luca2010/luca.html. For appeals procedures, see U.S. Office of Management and Budget, U.S. Department of Commerce, Bureau of the Census, "Procedures for Participating in the Appeals Process for the 2010 Decennial Census Local Update of Census Addresses (LUCA) Program; Notice," 74 *Federal Register* 47424-47429, September 15, 2009.

[85] Testimony of then-Census Bureau Director Steve Murdock in U.S. Congress, House Committee on Oversight and Government Reform, Subcommittee on Information Policy, Census, and National Archives, *The 2010 Census Communications Campaign*, hearing, 110th Cong., 2nd sess., July 10, 2008 (Washington: 2008), pp. 4-5.

[86] U.S. Bureau of the Census, "Census in Schools," http://www.census.gov/schools/.

[87] Testimony of then-Acting Census Bureau Director Thomas Mesenbourg in U.S. Congress, House Committee on Oversight and Government Reform, Subcommittee on Information Policy, Census, and National Archives, *Census 2010: Assessing the Bureau's Strategies for Reducing the Undercount of Hard-to-Count Populations*, hearing, 111th Cong., 1st sess., March 23, 2009 (Washington: 2009), pp. 3-4.

[88] U.S. Government Accountability Office, *2010 Census: Data Collection Is Under Way, but Reliability of Key Information Technology Systems Remains a Risk*, GAO-10-567T, March 25, 2010, p. 18.

[89] Testimony of Associate Census Bureau Director Arnold Jackson in U.S. Congress, House Committee on Oversight and Government Reform, Subcommittee on Information Policy, Census, and National Archives, *2010 Census: A Status Update of Key Decennial Operations*, March 25, 2010, p. 5, http://www.census.gov/newsroom/releases/pdf/AAJ_Testimony_3-25-10.pdf.

[90] Ibid. See also testimony of then-Census Bureau Director Steve Murdock in U.S. Congress, House Committee on Oversight and Government Reform, Subcommittee on Information Policy, Census, and National Archives, *The 2010 Census Communications Campaign*, hearing, 110th Cong., 2nd sess., July 10, 2008 (Washington: 2008), p. 5.

[91] College dormitories, nursing homes, and prisons, along with military barracks, are examples of group quarters noted previously in this report. U.S. Government Accountability Office, *2010 Census: Cooperation with Enumerators Is Critical to a Successful Headcount*, GAO-10-665T, April 30, 2010, p. 3.

[92] U.S. Government Accountability Office, *2010 Census: Data Collection Is Under Way, but Reliability of Key Information Technology Systems Remains a Risk*, GAO-10-567T, March 25, 2010, p. 19.

[93] Ibid., pp. 22-23.

[94] Testimony of Associate Census Bureau Director Arnold Jackson in U.S. Congress, House Committee on Oversight and Government Reform, Subcommittee on Information Policy, Census, and National Archives, *2010 Census: A Status Update of Key Decennial Operations*, March 25, 2010, p. 4, http://www.census.gov/newsroom/releases/pdf/AAJ_Testimony_3-25-10.pdf.

[95] U.S. Government Accountability Office, *2010 Census: Census Bureau Should Take Action to Improve the Credibility and Accuracy of Its Cost Estimate for the Decennial Census*, GAO-08-554, June 2008, p. 16.

[96] U.S. Government Accountability Office, *2010 Census: Data Collection Is Under Way, but Reliability of Key Information Technology Systems Remains a Risk*, GAO-10-567T, March 25, 2010, p. 11.

[97] Ibid., pp. 11-12.

[98] Ibid., p. 11.

[99] Ibid., p. 12.

[100] See, for example, Jonathan Allen, "White House to Bypass Commerce—and Gregg—on Census," CQ Today Online News, CQ.com, February 5, 2009, 5:54 a.m., http://www.cq.com/document/display.do?dockey=/cqonline/prod/data/docs/html/news/111/news111-000003024858.html@allnews& metapub= CQ-NEWS&binderName=latest-news-binder&seqNum=13.

[101] H.R. 1254, 111th Congress, introduced on February 3, 2009, by Rep. Maloney and referred to the House Oversight and Government Reform Committee, Information Policy, Census, and National Archives Subcommittee, would have removed the Census Bureau from the Commerce Department and made it an independent establishment. The Director would have been a presidential appointee with a five-year term of office. Two other proposals would have kept the Bureau in the Commerce Department, but given the Director a five-year term and somewhat greater autonomy within DOC than is now the case. The measures were H.R. 4945, which Rep. Maloney introduced on March 25, 2010, and S. 3167, a companion bill introduced the same day by Sen. Carper. The House bill was referred to the Oversight and Government Reform Committee. S. 3167, referred to the Homeland Security and Governmental Affairs Committee, Federal Financial Management, Government Information, Federal Services, and International Security Subcommittee, was ordered to be reported favorably, as amended, on April 28, 2010. The Senate passed S. 3167 on December 8, 2010, but the bill failed in the House on December 14, 2010.

[102] See, as examples, Jonathan Allen, "White House: Census Director to 'Work Closely' with West Wing," *CQ Today Online News*, CQ.com, February 5, 2009, 6:34 p.m., http://www.cq.com/document/display.do?dockey=/cqonline/prod/data/docs/html/news/111/news111-000003025792.html@allnews&metapub=CQ-NEWS &binderName= latest-news-binder&seq Num=12; and Keith Koffler, "Census Control Clarified," *Roll Call*, March 11, 2009, pp. 1, 22.

[103] Testimony of Gary Locke in U.S. Congress, Senate Committee on Commerce, Science, and Transportation, *Nomination of Gary Locke to Be U.S. Secretary of Commerce*, hearing, 111th Cong., 1st sess., March 18, 2009 (Washington: 2009), p. 2.

[104] Testimony of Robert M. Groves in U.S. Congress, Senate Committee on Homeland Security and Governmental Affairs, *Nomination of Robert M. Groves to Be Director of the Census*,

hearing, 111th Cong., 1st sess., May 15, 2009 (Washington: 2009). For the full text of his opening remarks, see http://hsgac.senate.gov/public/_files/ 051509Groves.pdf.

[105] See Allan Holmes, "Census program to use handheld computers said to be in 'serious trouble'," GovernmentExecutive.com, January 2, 2008, http://www.govexec.com /story_page.cfm? filepath=/ dailyfed/0108/ 010208h1.htm. This article contained a link to MITRE's November 29, 2007, "Talking Points for Meeting with [then-Census Bureau Deputy Director] Jay Waite."

[106] See Committee on National Statistics, "About CNSTAT," http://www7.national academies.org/cnstat/ What%20is%20CNSTAT.html.

[107] See, as examples, Lawrence D. Brown, Michael L. Cohen, et al., *Experimentation and Evaluation Plans for the 2010 Census* (Washington: National Academies Press, 2008); and Robert M. Bell and Michael L. Cohen, eds., *Coverage Measurement in the 2010 Census* (Washington: National Academies Press, 2009).

[108] The Board's presidential members and congressional members prepared separate final reports, both dated September 1, 2001.

In: The 2010 Census: Operations and Outcomes   ISBN: 978-1-61324-348-0
Editors: K. De Luca and C. Moretti   © 2011 Nova Science Publishers, Inc.

Chapter 2

2010 CENSUS: DATA COLLECTION OPERATIONS WERE GENERALLY COMPLETED AS PLANNED, BUT LONG-STANDING CHALLENGES SUGGEST NEED FOR FUNDAMENTAL REFORMS[*]

United States Government Accountability Office

WHY GAO DID THIS STUDY

Although the U.S. Census Bureau (Bureau) generally completed the field data collection phase of the 2010 Census consistent with its operational plans, at $13 billion, 2010 was the costliest census in the nation's history. Moving forward, it will be important to both refine existing operations as well as to reexamine the fundamental approach to the census to better address long-standing issues such as securing participation and escalating costs. As requested, this report reviews (1) the conduct of nonresponse follow-up (NRFU), where enumerators collect data from households that did not return their census forms, (2) the implementation of other field operations critical to a complete count, and (3) potential reexamination areas that could help produce a more cost-effective 2020 Census. The report is based on GAO's analysis of

---

[*] This is an edited, reformatted and augmented version of United States Government Accountability Office publication GAO-11-193, dated December 2010.

Bureau data and documents, surveys of local census office managers, and field observations.

WHAT GAO RECOMMENDS

GAO recommends that the Census Director refine NRFU and other field follow-up efforts by, among other things, emphasizing quality as much as speed during NRFU and by incorporating best practices in its IT acquisition-management policy. To help ensure reform efforts stay on track, the Bureau should develop an operational plan that integrates performance, budget, and other information. The Department of Commerce generally agreed with GAO's findings and recommendations.

WHAT GAO FOUND

Nationally, the Bureau was well positioned to implement NRFU and subsequent field operations. The Bureau achieved a mail response rate of 63 percent, which was within its expectations, and recruited nearly 3.8 million total applicants for census jobs, which was 104 percent of its staffing goal. Moreover, the Bureau completed NRFU under budget, reportedly spending $1.59 billion on the operation, about $660 million (29 percent) less than the Bureau initially estimated. Most of the Bureau's local census offices (LCO) also completed NRFU ahead of the 10-week allotted time frame. Despite these operational successes, the Bureau encountered some notable challenges. For example, the pace of NRFU may have fostered a culture that tended to emphasize speed over quality, as those LCOs with higher percentages of less-complete questionnaires were more likely to have completed NRFU in 53 days or less (the average time LCOs took to complete NRFU). The Bureau also had to overcome issues with critical information technology (IT) systems. For example, performance problems with the IT system used to manage NRFU led to processing backlogs. Although the Bureau developed workarounds for the issue, it hindered the Bureau's ability to fully implement quality-assurance procedures as planned.

The Bureau generally completed other follow-up operations designed to improve the accuracy of the data consistent with its plans. One of these activities was the vacant/delete check (VDC), where enumerators verified housing units thought to be vacant or nonexistent. The Bureau completed VDC two days ahead of schedule, but encountered duplicate addresses on the address list used for the operation, which could indicate a more systemic problem with the quality of the Bureau's address list.

While it will be important to refine existing census-taking activities—many of which have been in place since 1970—results of prior censuses point to the fact that simply improving current methods will not bring about the reforms needed to control costs and maintain accuracy. The cost of conducting the census has, on average, doubled each decade since 1970. At the same time, because of demographic and attitudinal trends, securing a complete count has become an increasing challenge. As a result, a fundamental reexamination of the nation's approach to the census will be needed for a more cost-effective enumeration in 2020. Potential focus areas include new data collection methods; the tenure of the Census Director; and ensuring the Bureau's approaches to human-capital management, knowledge sharing, and other internal functions are aligned toward delivering more cost-effective outcomes. The Bureau recognizes that fundamental changes are needed and has already taken some important first steps, including developing a strategic plan. To help ensure the Bureau's efforts stay on track and to avoid problems it had in planning for prior censuses, it will be important for the Bureau to issue a comprehensive operational plan that includes performance goals, milestones, cost estimates, and other critical information that could be updated regularly.

ABBREVIATIONS

AA	assignment area
Bureau	U.S. Census Bureau
CCM	census coverage measurement
FBI	Federal Bureau of Investigation
IT	information technology
LCO	local census office
MaRCS	Matching Review and Coding System
NPC	National Processing Center
NRFU	nonresponse follow-up
PBOCS	Paper-Based Operations Control System
PI	person interviewing
VDC	vacant/delete check

14, 2010
The Honorable Thomas R. Carper
Chairman
The Honorable John McCain
Ranking Member
Subcommittee on Federal Financial Management, Government Information, Federal Services, and International Security
Committee on Homeland Security and Governmental Affairs
United States Senate

The Honorable Darrell E. Issa
Ranking Member
Committee on Oversight and Government Reform
House of Representatives

The Honorable Wm. Lacy Clay
Chairman
The Honorable Patrick T. McHenry
Ranking Member
Subcommittee on Information Policy, Census and National Archives
Committee on Oversight and Government Reform
House of Representatives

One of the final acts of the decade-long census life cycle is to occur in the remaining days of 2010 when, as required by law, the U.S. Census Bureau (Bureau) is to release to the President the state population counts used to apportion Congress.[1] Although some additional work and more data releases lie ahead, and information on the accuracy of the count is not scheduled to be available until early 2012, this much is clear: the Bureau generally completed the enumeration phase of the 2010 Census on schedule and consistent with its operational plans, and largely surmounted a series of risks that jeopardized the success of the headcount.

As you know, an operationally successful census was no small accomplishment. Various social and demographic trends such as an increasingly diverse population and a distrust of government made a complete count an extraordinary challenge in 2010. At the same time, the Bureau had to overcome a variety of internal management challenges including shortcomings with critical information technology (IT) systems.

We have long reported that the decennial census is a shared national undertaking, where the Bureau, Congress, government agencies at all levels, private organizations, and ultimately the public at large, all play vital roles in securing a complete count. That the Bureau completed key operations on schedule, obtained an acceptable participation rate, and is on track for meeting legally mandated deadlines for reporting population figures is a tremendous credit to the people of this nation for completing their census forms and cooperating with enumerators; the hundreds of thousands of career and temporary Bureau employees who diligently implemented a vast array of census-taking activities, often under difficult circumstances; public, private, tribal, and nonprofit organizations of all sizes for voluntarily partnering with the Bureau and raising awareness of the census; and finally to Congress, which provided the necessary support while holding the Bureau accountable for results.

Despite these impressive achievements, the 2010 Census required an unprecedented commitment of resources, including recruiting more than 3.8 million total applicants—roughly equivalent to the entire population of Oregon—for its temporary workforce; and it escalated in cost from an initial estimate of $11.3 billion in 2001 to around $13 billion, the most expensive population count in our nation's history. Further, our oversight of the 1990, 2000, and now 2010 Censuses suggests that the fundamental design of the enumeration—in many ways unchanged since 1970—is no longer capable of delivering a cost-effective headcount given the nation's increasing diversity and other sociodemographic trends.

Indeed, beginning in 1990, we reported that rising costs, difficulties in securing public participation, and other long-standing challenges required a revised census methodology, a view that was shared by other stakeholders.[2] For 2010, the Bureau eliminated the long-form questionnaire in an effort to boost response rates, and refined other census-taking activities, but the basic approach to the enumeration is essentially the same as it was 40 years ago, and achieving acceptable results using these conventional methods has required an increasingly larger investment of fiscal resources, resources that in the coming years will become increasingly scarce.

In short, as the nation turns the corner on the 2010 Census, it will be vitally important to both identify lessons learned from the current decennial census to improve existing census-taking activities, as well as to reexamine and perhaps fundamentally transform the way the Bureau plans, tests, implements, monitors, and evaluates future enumerations in order to address long-standing challenges.

As requested, this report assesses the implementation of (1) nonresponse follow-up (NRFU), the largest and most costly census field operation, where the Bureau sends enumerators to collect data from households that did not mail back their census forms, and (2) other key follow-up field operations that were critical for ensuring a complete count; and (3) identifies key questions and focus areas that will be important for the Bureau, Congress, and census stakeholders to consider going forward now that planning for the next enumeration is underway.

This report is one of three we are releasing today. Among the other two, one focuses on the Bureau's efforts to reach out to and enumerate hard-to-count populations, while the other examines the implementation of operations aimed at reducing census coverage errors. Both reports identify preliminary lessons learned, as well as potential focus areas for improvement.[3]

In reviewing NRFU, we examined the pace of production, the fingerprinting of census workers as part of a background check, and the performance of a critical automated system. The follow-up operations we reviewed for this report include the vacant/delete check (VDC), where the Bureau verifies the status of housing units flagged earlier in the census as being unoccupied or nonexistent; and census coverage measurement (CCM), where the Bureau assesses the completeness and accuracy of the census count.

For all three objectives, we (1) analyzed Bureau cost and progress data as well as planning and other pertinent documents; (2) conducted periodic surveys of the Bureau's 494 local census office (LCO) managers using a series of online questionnaires that asked about their experience in managing LCO activities; and (3) made field observations at 28 locations across the country selected for various factors such as their geographic and demographic diversity, and including parts of such urban areas as Atlanta, Boston, Chicago, Detroit, New Orleans, New York City, San Francisco, and Tucson, as well as less-populated areas such as Meridian, Mississippi, and New Castle, Delaware. We also interviewed Bureau officials at headquarters and LCO managers and staff, and reviewed our prior work on the planning and implementation of the 1990, 2000, and 2010 Censuses. Moreover, to help inform a reexamination of the nation's approach to the census, in addition to the above, we reviewed our prior work on governmentwide reexamination, as well as leading practices and attributes in the areas of IT management, organizational performance, collaboration, stewardship, and human capital.[4] Appendix I includes additional information on our scope and methodology and a list of LCOs we visited. Data presented in this report measuring operational timeliness and data quality were drawn from Bureau management and operational data systems. To assess the reliability of the data, we reviewed Bureau electronic documentation to gain information about the data and their sources, and followed up with agency officials knowledgeable about the data in cases where we had questions about potential errors or inconsistencies. On the basis of our efforts, we determined that the data were sufficiently reliable for the purposes of supporting the findings and recommendations in this report.

We conducted this performance audit from December 2009 until December 2010 in accordance with generally accepted government auditing standards. Those standards require that we plan and perform the audits to obtain sufficient, appropriate evidence to provide a reasonable basis for our findings and conclusions based on our audit objectives. We believe that the evidence obtained provides a reasonable basis for our findings and conclusions based on our audit objectives.

On December 7, 2010, the Secretary of Commerce provided written comments on a draft of this report (see app. II). The Department of Commerce generally agreed with the overall findings and recommendations of the report. In addition, the Secretary of Commerce provided the Bureau's technical comments and suggestions where additional context might be needed, and we revised the report to reflect these comments where appropriate.

BACKGROUND

The decennial census is a constitutionally mandated enterprise critical to our nation. Census data are used to apportion congressional seats, redraw congressional districts, and help allocate hundreds of billions of dollars in federal aid to state and local governments each year. A complete count of the nation's population is an enormous challenge requiring the successful alignment of thousands of activities, hundreds of thousands of temporary employees, and millions of forms. Indeed, over the past year, in an effort to secure a complete count, the Bureau mailed out questionnaires to about 120 million housing units for occupants to complete and mail back; hand-delivered approximately 12 million questionnaires—mostly in rural locations as well as in areas along the Gulf Coast affected by recent hurricanes—for residents to fill out and return by mail; went door-to-door collecting data from the approximately 46.6 million households that did not mail back their census forms; and conducted operations aimed at counting people in less-conventional dwellings such as migrant-worker housing, boats, tent cities, homeless shelters, nursing homes, dormitories, and prisons. In short, the decennial census is large, logistically complex, and, at a cost now estimated at around $13 billion, expensive.

In developing the 2010 Census, the Bureau faced three significant internal challenges: critical IT systems had performance problems during testing, cost-estimates lacked precision, and some key operations were not tested under census-like conditions. These were some of the issues that led us to designate the 2010 Census a GAO high-risk area in 2008.[5]

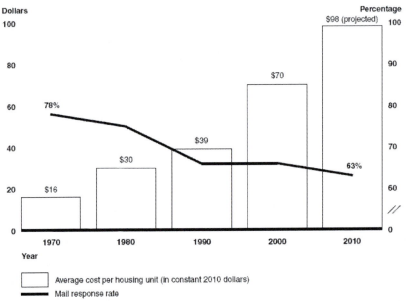

Source: GAO analysis of Census Bureau data.

Note: In the 2010 Census the Bureau used only a short-form questionnaire. For this report we use the 1990 and 2000 Census short-form mail response rate when comparing 1990, 2000, and 2010 mail-back response rates. Census short-form mail response rates are unavailable for 1970 and 1980, so we use the overall response rate.

Figure 1. The Average Cost of Counting Each Housing Unit (in Constant 2010 Dollars) Has Escalated Each Decade While Mail Response Rates Have Declined.

Although every census has its decade-specific difficulties, sociodemographic trends such as concerns over personal privacy, more non-English speakers, and more people residing in makeshift and other nontraditional living arrangements make each decennial increasingly challenging and do not bode well for the cost-effectiveness of future counts.

As shown in figure 1, the cost of enumerating each housing unit has escalated from around $16 in 1970 to around $98 in 2010, in constant 2010 dollars (an increase of over 500 percent). At the same time, the mail response rate—a key indicator of a successful census—has declined from 78 percent in 1970 to 63 percent in 2010. The mail response rate is an important figure because it determines the NRFU workload and ultimately, NRFU costs. In many ways, the Bureau has to invest substantially more resources each decade just to match the prior decennial's response rate.

In our earlier work on high-performing organizations, we noted that the federal government must confront a range of new challenges to enhance performance, ensure accountability, and position the nation for the future.[6] Nothing less than a fundamental transformation in the people, processes, technology, and environment used by federal agencies to address public goals will be necessary to address public needs. Ultimately, however, the federal government needs to change its culture to be more results-oriented. For the Bureau, as with all federal agencies, this means ensuring, among other things, that its culture embraces results rather than outputs; follows matrixes rather than stovepipes; forms partnerships rather than protecting turf; focuses on risk management rather than risk avoidance; and takes proactive approaches rather than behaving reactively.

NRFU WAS GENERALLY SUCCESSFUL; REFINEMENTS COULD IMPROVE PROCEDURES FOR 2020

The Bureau Met Its Response Rate Goal, but Recruited More Enumerators than Needed and Should Revisit Its Staffing Model

Nationally, in terms of workload (as determined by the mail response rate) and staffing levels, the Bureau was well positioned to implement NRFU. With respect to the response rate, the Bureau expected a level of 59 percent to 65 percent. The actual mail response rate on April 19, when the Bureau initially determined the universe of houses to visit for NRFU, was just over 63 percent, well within the Bureau's range of estimates. This translated into an initial workload of 48.6 million housing units.

Achieving this response rate was an important accomplishment as the nation's population is growing steadily larger, more diverse, and according to the Bureau, increasingly difficult to find and reluctant to participate in the census. High response rates are essential because they save taxpayer dollars. According to the Bureau, for every 1 percentage point increase in mail response in 2010, the Bureau saved $85 million that would otherwise have been spent on the follow-up efforts. According to the Bureau, it costs 42 cents to mail back each census form in a postage-paid envelope, compared with an average estimate of around $57 for field activities necessary to enumerate each housing unit in person. Moreover, mail returns tend to have better-quality data, in part because as time goes on after Census Day (April 1), people move, or may have difficulty recalling who was residing with them.

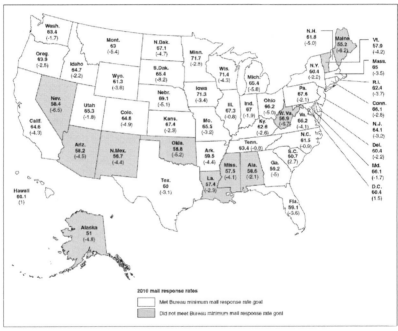

Source: GAO analysis of preliminary Census Bureau data; Map Resources (map).
Note: Number in bold reflects the 2010 response rate as of April 19, 2010. Number below in parentheses reflects the percentage change in response rate from 2000 to 2010. 2000 response rate as of April 18, 2000.

Figure 2. The Bureau Met Its Minimum Mail Response Rate Goal of 59 Percent in All but 11 States, but Rates Generally Declined Compared to 2000.

As illustrated in figure 2, the Bureau met its expected response rate in all but 11 states. The highest response rate (71.7 percent) was in Minnesota, while the lowest response rate (51 percent) was in Alaska. At the same time, response rates in all but two states—Hawaii and South Carolina—as well as the District of Columbia, declined anywhere from 0.8 to 8.2 percentage points when compared to 2000, thus underscoring the difficulty the Bureau will face in the future in trying to sustain response rates.[7] The mail response rate is important because it helps the Bureau determine the housing units that failed to mail back the census questionnaires, and thus are included in the NRFU workload.

The mail response rate differs from the participation rate in that it is calculated as a percentage of all housing units in the mail-back universe, including those that are later found to be nonexistent or unoccupied. In contrast, the participation rate is the percentage of forms mailed back by households that received them and is a better measure of cooperation with the census. According to a Bureau press release dated October 21, 2010, the nation achieved a final mail participation rate of 74 percent, matching the final mail participation rate that was achieved for the 2000 Census. Compared to 2000, participation rates for 22 states and the District of Columbia, either met or exceeded their 2000 Census rate.

Key factors aimed at improving the mail response rate included the mailing of an advance letter, a reminder postcard, and an aggressive marketing and outreach program. In addition, this is the first decennial census the Bureau sent a second or "replacement" questionnaire to households. Replacement questionnaires were sent to around 25 million households in census tracts that had the lowest response rates in the 2000 Census, and 10 million replacement questionnaires were sent to nonresponding households in other census tracts that had low-tomoderate response rates in 2000.

With respect to staffing levels, the Bureau set a recruitment goal of nearly 3.7 million total applicants and achieved 104 percent of this goal by April 25, 2010, recruiting more than 3.8 million total applicants, almost a week prior to the start of NRFU (once the Bureau had an adequate pool of candidates for 2010, it attempted to limit the number of additional applicants, taking such steps as discontinuing the advertising of census jobs in mailed-out census materials).

According to the Bureau, based on past experience, it set its recruiting goal at five times the number of persons that needed to be trained to ensure it had an ample pool of candidates in specific areas with specific skills, as well as to ensure it had a sufficient supply of enumerators during the course of its field operations. The Bureau's approach was similar to that used for the 2000 Census despite vast differences in the economy. During the 2000 Census, the Bureau was recruiting in the midst of one of the tightest labor markets in nearly three decades. In contrast, during the 2010 Census, the Bureau was recruiting workers during a period of high unemployment. While having too few enumerators could affect the Bureau's ability to complete NRFU on schedule, overrecruiting has its own costs. For example, there are costs associated with administering and processing the test taken at the time an individual applies for a census job, as well as a $2 charge to have a name background check run on all applicants. Overrecruiting can also be burdensome on applicants as they need to find a test site and take a test before they can be hired for a census job—a job that because the Bureau has overrecruited, may not be available. In looking forward to 2020, it will be important for the Bureau to more precisely refine its recruiting model based on lessons learned from the labor markets in both 2000 and 2010, and use this information to develop more accurate recruiting targets. It will also be important for the Bureau to adhere to recruiting goals so that additional costs are not incurred.

The Bureau Completed NRFU $660 Million under Budget

The Bureau budgeted that NRFU would cost around $2.25 billion. However, by the end of the operation, the Bureau reported using approximately $1.59 billion, which was 29 percent lower than budgeted. The Bureau, with congressional approval, also set up a contingency fund of $574 million to cover additional expenses that could have been caused by unfavorable weather and other unforeseen events. However, in the end, contingency money was not needed to complete NRFU.

While the Bureau conducted NRFU under budget, the difference between actual and expected NRFU costs also highlights the need for the Bureau to develop an accurate cost model in order to establish more credible cost estimates for 2020. In addition to NRFU, other census operations had substantial variances between their initial cost estimates and their actual costs. In our 2008 report, we noted that the Bureau had insufficient policies and procedures and inadequately trained staff for conducting high-quality cost estimation for the decennial census, and recommended that the Bureau take a variety of steps to improve the credibility and accuracy of its cost estimates, including performing sensitivity and uncertainty analyses.[8] The Bureau generally agreed with our recommendation and is taking steps to address them.

Most Local Census Offices Finished NRFU ahead of Schedule, but the Bureau's Ambitious Production Schedule May Have Produced Mixed Results

In conducting NRFU, it is important for enumerators to follow Bureau procedures for collecting complete and accurate data while keeping production on schedule so that subsequent activities can begin as planned. Timely completion of NRFU is also important because as time goes on, people move or might have difficulty remembering who was living in a household on Census Day.

The Bureau went to great lengths to obtain complete data directly from household members. For example, Bureau procedures generally called for enumerators to make six attempts to reach each household on different days of the week at different times until they obtained needed information on that household. However, in cases where household members could not be contacted or refused to answer all or part of the census questionnaire, enumerators were permitted to obtain data via proxy (a neighbor, building manager, or other nonhousehold member presumed to know about its residents), or if an enumerator after the required six attempts was unable to collect data from either the household or a proxy respondent then the enumerator submitted the incomplete questionnaire to the LCO (this is referred to as a "closeout interview"). Closeout interviews are processed at Bureau headquarters where statistical methods are used to determine household information.

For the 2010 Census, NRFU began May 1 and was scheduled to finish July 10, 2010. However, a majority of LCOs generally finished their NRFU workloads ahead of this 10-week time frame. For example, by June 28, 2010, week 8 of the NRFU operation, 342 of the Bureau's 494 LCOs (almost 69 percent), had completed 100 percent of their workload. Figure 3 shows the production levels over the course of NRFU.

A number of factors helped most LCOs complete NRFU ahead of schedule. For example, the Bureau removed almost 2 million late mail returns prior to the start of NRFU, reducing the follow-up workload from 48.6 million to 46.6 million housing units (a 4 percent reduction in NRFU workload). The removal of the late mail returns resulted in a 1.5 percent increase in mail response rate, saving approximately $127.5 million (based on the Bureau's estimate that a 1 percentage point increase in the mail response rate would decrease workload costs by around $85 million).

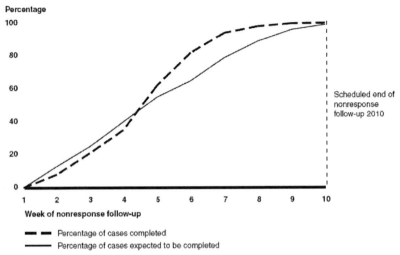

Source: GAO analysis of Census Bureau data.

Figure 3. The Expected and Actual Number of Cases Completed during NRFU.

Another factor that was instrumental to the success of NRFU was retaining a sufficiently skilled workforce. Because of high unemployment rates, turnover was far lower than anticipated. Advertising census jobs locally helped to ensure an adequate number of applicants, and according to the Bureau, mileage reimbursement may have been lower, in part because enumerators lived in and had local knowledge about the neighborhoods they were assigned. Further, people may have been more willing to cooperate with enumerators who were from their own community. For example, at a Native American village in New Mexico, local enumerators were aware that according to the community's customs it was considered offensive to launch into business without first engaging in conversation. In addition, local enumerators in hurricane-affected rural areas of Louisiana were able to successfully locate households based on their knowledge of the geography. For example, based on his familiarity with the area, one enumerator we observed was able to locate an assigned household not included on a census map using only a brief description, such as "a white house with green roof away from the road."

The Bureau also used weekly production goals that helped LCOs focus on the need to stay on schedule and to track their progress. However, several measures we reviewed underscored the challenge that LCOs faced in hitting these production goals while still maintaining data quality.

Significantly, our analysis of Bureau data found that the fast pace of NRFU was associated with the collection of less-complete household data.[9] Indeed, after controlling for such variables as response rate and local enumeration challenges, we found that LCOs with higher percentages of proxy interviews and closeout interviews were more likely to have finished NRFU in 53 days or less (the average amount of time LCOs took to complete their NRFU workloads) compared to LCOs with lower percentages of proxy and closeout interviews. As noted above, proxy interviews contain data provided by a nonhousehold member (e.g., a neighbor) and may thus be less reliable than information collected directly from a household member, while a closeout interview is one where no interview is conducted and household information is later determined using statistical methods at Bureau headquarters during data processing.

The pace of NRFU and its potential effect on data quality was also reflected in the responses of a number of LCO managers we surveyed. For example, although almost half of the LCO managers responding to our survey said they were satisfied with their ability to meet production goals while maintaining data quality, almost 30 percent of respondents were dissatisfied with their ability to meet production goals while maintaining data quality (around 20 percent responded that they were neither satisfied nor dissatisfied). Some of the LCO managers commented that they felt undue pressure to finish the operation early (sometimes a month earlier than planned) and as a result, finishing early could have come at the expense of accuracy. In one example, an LCO manager noted that it appeared as though the LCOs were in a race to finish NRFU as fast as possible, even if the best data were not received. Another LCO manager said that even though his office was surpassing the daily production goals, he was still being pressured to finish faster, and that accuracy was not mentioned. Also, LCO managers expressed frustration at production goals being changed frequently or unexpectedly moved earlier.

Further, during our field visits, some LCO managers we spoke with at the start of NRFU were concerned about meeting production goals as there were not enough assignment area (AA) binders containing maps and address registers for every enumerator due to problems with the Bureau's Paper-Based Operations Control System (PBOCS), a key IT system that we discuss below. To ensure that enumerators had sufficient work, some crew leaders split-up AA binders between two or more enumerators. This is contrary to Bureau procedures which require enumerators to have their own AA binder. When the binders are split, only one enumerator has the required maps. Without maps an enumerator is unable to determine an assignment area's boundaries and ensure that the locations of all housing units are accurately recorded, which can affect data quality.

Later in NRFU, managers at two LCOs we visited said they felt pressure to finish NRFU ahead of schedule. At one LCO, managers explained that the regional office wanted to finish NFRU by June 12, or approximately 4 weeks ahead of schedule. However, at that LCO they were only 85 percent complete by week 5, and because NRFU procedures instruct enumerators to make up to six attempts to contact a household, they were not sure how they were going to finish by week 5 without having to accept more refusals and incomplete interviews—leading to potentially more proxy and closeout interviews, thus reducing data quality.

At the other LCO, production goals were stretched 15 percentage points above the national goal in order to complete NRFU ahead of schedule. One of the field supervisors at that office told us that he was able to meet the revised production goals by having enumerators share their workload. For example, in the morning, one enumerator would work the AA, and any remaining cases were given to another enumerator in the evening to complete. While this approach might have enhanced efficiency, the sharing of enumerator assignments makes it more difficult for the Bureau's quality-assurance procedures to identify enumerators that are not following procedures and may need to be retrained. Under the Bureau's procedures, AAs are to be assigned to one enumerator at a time.

In late-May 2010, while NRFU was still underway, we discussed the pace of the operation with Bureau officials, and whether enumerators were more often accepting less-complete household information. In response, Bureau officials notified the LCOs and reminded them of the importance of following prescribed procedures. Moving forward, as the Bureau conducts its evaluations of its 2010 NRFU operation and begins planning for 2020, it will be important for Bureau officials to closely examine the quality of data collected during NRFU and the pace of the operation, and determine whether it is placing appropriate emphasis on both objectives.

The Bureau Improved Its Procedures for Fingerprinting Employees, but More Work Is Needed

To better screen its workforce of hundreds of thousands of temporary census workers, the Bureau fingerprinted its temporary workforce for the first time in the 2010 Census.[10] In past censuses, temporary workers were only subject to a name background check that was completed at the time of recruitment. The Bureau, however, encountered problems capturing fingerprints during address canvassing, an operation that the Bureau conducted in the summer of 2009 to verify every address in the country. According to the Bureau, 22 percent of the approximately 162,000 workers hired for address canvassing had unclassifiable prints, or fingerprints that were incomplete or unreadable. The Federal Bureau of Investigation (FBI) determined that this problem was generally the result of errors that occurred when the prints were first taken at the LCOs that affected the readability of the two fingerprint cards that were created for each individual.

To address these problems, the Bureau improved its training procedures and purchased additional equipment in order to fingerprint some 580,000 NRFU temporary employees. Specifically, the Bureau refined training manuals used to instruct LCO staff on how to take fingerprints, scheduled fingerprint training closer to when the prints were captured, and increased the length of training. Further, the Bureau used an oil-free lotion during fingerprinting that is believed to raise the ridges on fingertips to improve the legibility of the prints.

Source: GAO (May 2010).

Figure 4. Digital Fingerprint Scanner.

The Bureau also revised its procedures to digitally capture a third and fourth set of fingerprints when the first two sets of fingerprint cards could not be read. The Bureau purchased around a thousand digital fingerprint scanners (see fig. 4) for this new effort. The Bureau estimated that this additional step could reduce the percentage of temporary workers with unclassifiable prints from 22 percent to approximately 10 to 12 percent, or an estimated 60,000 to 72,000 temporary workers for NRFU. As of May 25, 2010, it reduced the percentage of temporary workers with unclassifiable prints to 8.6 percent of 635,251, or approximately 54,000 temporary workers.

Fingerprint cards were sent from each LCO to the Bureau's National Processing Center (NPC) in Indiana where they were scanned and sent to the FBI. We visited the NPC during peak processing and observed that NPC was able to adequately handle the workload without any glitches. However, capturing fingerprints at training sites did not go as well. Some LCOs mentioned that collecting fingerprints took more time than expected, thus reducing the time available for enumerator field training. In our observations, at one LCO it took an extra 2 hours to fingerprint enumerators, and at another fingerprinting took so long it carried over to the next day (which put the NRFU instructor behind schedule). Furthermore, almost 50 percent of LCO managers responding to our survey reported dissatisfaction with fingerprinting procedures, compared to about 30 percent of LCO managers who were satisfied. For example, LCO managers commented that they did not have enough time to train staff conducting the fingerprinting or did not have adequate fingerprinting supplies, such as cards and ink pads. Several LCO managers said that the process was time-consuming, yet the additional time spent did not produce higher-quality prints, possibly because staff did not have fingerprinting expertise. Although some LCO managers said they would have preferred more digital fingerprinting, others reported that the digital fingerprint scanners did not work well and were time-consuming to use. In looking forward to 2020, the Bureau should revise or modify training so that field staff are provided with numerous practice opportunities for collecting fingerprints prior to each operation.

Workarounds Helped Mitigate PBOCS Issues, but Continuing Problems Hampered the Implementation of Key Quality-Assurance Procedures

Since 2005, we have reported on weaknesses in the Bureau's management and testing of key 2010 Census IT systems. Although the IT systems ultimately functioned well enough for the Bureau to carry out the census, workarounds developed to address performance problems with PBOCS— a workflow-management system crucial for the Bureau's field operations— adversely affected the Bureau's ability to implement key quality-assurance procedures as planned.

In June 2005, we noted that the Bureau had not fully implemented key practices important to managing IT, including investment management, system development and management, and enterprise architecture[11] management.[12] As a result, we concluded that the Bureau's IT investmentswere at increased risk of mismanagement, and were more likely to experience cost and schedule overruns and performance shortfalls.

As development of the IT systems progressed, these problems were realized. For example, the Field Data Collection Automation program, which included the development of handheld computers to collect information for address canvassing and NRFU, experienced substantial schedule delays and cost increases.[13] As a result, the Bureau later decided to abandon the planned use of handheld data collection devices for NRFU and reverted to paper questionnaires. The Bureau developed PBOCS to manage the operation. However, as we stated in several testimonies, even with the approach of Census Day, PBOCS had not demonstrated the ability to function reliably under full operational loads required to complete NRFU.[14] We noted that the limited amount of time remaining to improve its reliability before it would be needed for key operations created a substantial challenge for the Bureau.

Although the Bureau worked aggressively to improve PBOCS performance, the system experienced significant issues at the start of NRFU. For example, despite efforts to upgrade its hardware and software, PBOCS continued to experience system outages, slow performance, and problems generating and maintaining timely progress reports. The Bureau has attributed these issues, in part, to the compressed development and testing schedule, as well as to inadequate performance and interface testing.

To mitigate the system's performance issues, the Bureau implemented various workarounds. For example, the Bureau frequently restricted the number of hours that PBOCS was available to users in order to implement software upgrades and perform other system maintenance activities. In addition, the Bureau restricted the number of concurrent PBOCS users at each LCO to help reduce demand on the system. These restrictions often limited the number of concurrent users to 3 to 5 users per LCO, or about 1,500 to 2,500 total users. According to a Bureau official with responsibility for PBOCS, the system was originally intended to provide access for over 7,000 concurrent users. While these workarounds improved the reliability of PBOCS, LCO managers who responded to our survey were consistently dissatisfied with the restrictions on the number of users allowed at one time, and many commented that the restrictions adversely affected their ability to keep up with the workload. Further, the limitations on the number of concurrent users, combined with PBOCS outages and slow performance, delayed the shipping of questionnaires to the data capture centers and resulted in a peak backlog of nearly 12 million questionnaires at the LCOs.

The substantial backlog of questionnaires hampered the Bureau's ability to effectively monitor productivity and data quality during NRFU as planned. Nearly 75 percent of LCO manager survey respondents were dissatisfied with the usefulness of PBOCS reports to plan and monitor work during NRFU. A dissatisfied respondent wrote in that the unavailability of reports greatly hampered his LCO's ability to conduct NRFU in an efficient manner. Almost 80 percent of responding LCO managers indicated that their LCO needed to put forth a substantial amount of extra effort to manually prepare reports to track productivity outside of PBOCS. The use of manual processes increased costs at the LCOs and raised the risk of human error.

The backlog of questionnaires also hampered the Bureau's ability to conduct NRFU reinterviews, a quality-assurance operation designed to identify enumerators who intentionally or unintentionally produced data errors. PBOCS was to select a sample of cases from each enumerator's completed workload, and these cases would be reinterviewed by another enumerator. Once cases were selected, a quality-assurance enumerator attempted to reinterview the original NRFU respondents in an effort to verify that accurate data was collected during the initial NRFU interview.

However, the backlog of questionnaires delayed the selection of reinterview cases and, as a result, some could not be conducted. For example, in areas with large populations of college students, the Bureau conducted NRFU early in order to maximize the probability of enumerating people before they were likely to move out from where they were living on Census Day. In some of those cases, reinterviews could not be conducted since the students had moved out by the time an enumerator was given the case for reinterview. In addition, it also took longer to detect and retrain an enumerator with performance problems. For example, LCO staff reported to us that, because of the delay carrying out reinterviews, it was often too late to retrain enumerators because they had already finished their assignments and were released before the errors were identified. In cases where an enumerator had intentionally falsified work, the enumerator was supposed to be released and all his or her work was to be redone. However, because of the PBOCS delays, falsified cases were sometimes identified after the enumerator was finished with his or her assignment, requiring their entire assignment area to be reenumerated.

Identifying errors and falsifications early in the operation would have minimized the number of housing units that needed to be reworked and reduced the burden for respondents. For example, an LCO manager told us that her office was not able to detect an enumerator's falsification until after NRFU, when the enumerator had already moved on to the next operation, requiring the LCO to rework nearly 200 cases. According to our survey, approximately 30 percent of LCO managers who experienced backlogs reported that they had substantial difficulty detecting errors or fraudulent interviewing as a result of the backlog, while more than 20 percent reported moderate difficulty and nearly 50 percent reported slight to no difficulty detecting errors or fraudulent interviewing as a result of the backlog.

The implementation of various workarounds helped the Bureau successfully complete NRFU. However, the lack of a fully functioning PBOCS limited the Bureau's ability to effectively monitor productivity or implement quality-assurance procedures as documented in its operational plans.

More generally, as the Bureau prepares for 2020, among other actions it will be important for it to continue to improve its ability to manage its IT investments. Leading up to the 2010 Census, we made numerous recommendations to the Bureau to improve its IT management practices by implementing best practices in risk management, requirements development, and testing, as well as establishing an IT acquisition-management policy that incorporates best practices.[15] While the Bureau implemented many of our recommendations, it did not implement our broader recommendation to institutionalize these practices at the organizational level. The challenges experienced by the Bureau in acquiring and developing IT systems during the 2010 Census further demonstrate the importance of establishing and enforcing a rigorous IT acquisition management policy Bureau-wide. In addition, it will be important for the Bureau to improve its ability to consistently perform key

IT management practices, such as IT investment management, system development and management, and enterprise architecture management. The effective use of these practices can better ensure that future IT investments will be pursued in a way that optimizes mission performance.

KEY FOLLOW-UP OPERATIONS WERE GENERALLY COMPLETED AS PLANNED

Vacant/Delete Check Operation Finished ahead of Schedule but over Budget

To help ensure that people are counted only once and in the right place, as well as to collect complete and correct information about them, after NRFU the Bureau conducts a number of operations designed to improve the accuracy of the data. One of these operations is the VDC operation, where enumerators verified the Census Day status of vacant and deleted (nonexistent) housing units. VDC also attempts to enumerate late additions to the Bureau's address file, such as newly constructed housing, and units for which the mail-out questionnaire was returned blank or incomplete. The Bureau refers to these additional addresses as supplemental cases. VDC has the potential to boost the accuracy of the census, especially among traditionally undercounted populations. A similar operation in 2000 found that 22 percent of housing units previously identified as vacant, and 25 percent of those previously flagged for deletion, were indeed occupied. Changing the status of these units led to a net gain of 3.1 million people in the 2000 population count.

The Bureau completed the VDC operation on August 23, slightly ahead of the original planned completion date of August 25, but also over budget. The Bureau spent about $281 million on VDC, approximately 15 percent over its baseline budget of $244 million. Bureau officials we spoke to attributed the operation's progress to the retention of experienced NRFU staff for VDC. They noted that VDC staff were knowledgeable about procedures and the locations in which they worked, and required less training than they would have if they had been newly hired. With respect to the cost overruns, the Bureau is analyzing why VDC exceeded its budget. According to a Bureau official, additional costs may be related to VDC cases being located farther apart than expected (which would require more staff time and mileage reimbursement) and to enumerators adding more new addresses than expected.

The VDC workload of 8.7 million housing units (5.6 million units vacant or flagged for deletion, 2.9 million supplemental addresses, and 0.2 million additions during the operation) was substantially less than the Bureau's previous estimate of 10.4 to 15.4 million units. During our review we found that while the Bureau had updated its total cost estimates for VDC, it had not adjusted day-to-day cost and progress expectations for VDC to account for the reduced workload. Not having the most recent targets for VDC could have impeded the Bureau's ability to effectively monitor the progress of enumerators in the field. We discussed this with Bureau officials, and in mid-July they revised VDC cost and progress estimates to account for the smaller workload, as well as other changes, including an earlier start date and reduced staffing.

Further, during our field observations, LCO staff told us that some VDC supplemental addresses had already been enumerated as occupied units during NRFU. These supplemental addresses were slightly different from the NRFU addresses (e.g., 123 Main Street versus 123A Main Street) and appeared to be duplicate addresses. Duplicate addresses are supposed to be checked during field verification (an operation to confirm the existence of certain housing units added to the Bureau's address file) and should not have been in the VDC workload. Because the issue could indicate a nationwide problem, we notified Bureau officials, and in response they instituted a new procedure to identify and process duplicate addresses without making a follow-up visit to the housing unit. Identifying duplicate addresses before they get enumerated a second time is important because unnecessarily visiting a housing unit previously counted can reduce the accuracy of census data and will increase costs.

In order to assess the reasons why VDC ran over budget, and as recommended in our June 2008 report, it will be important for the Bureau to document lessons learned for cost elements whose actual costs differ from the estimate.[16] Knowing this will allow the Bureau to develop a more accurate cost estimate for VDC in 2020. In addition, to ensure the accuracy of data collected during VDC, it will be important for the Bureau to research how duplicates were inadvertently included in the VDC workload, as this data will help the Bureau compile a better address list for VDC operations in 2020.

Census Coverage Measurement Redesigned with Smaller Sample to Reduce Nonsampling Errors

The Bureau attempts to conduct a complete and accurate count of the nation's population; nonetheless, some degree of coverage error is inevitable because of the inherent complexity of counting the nation's large and diverse population and limitations in census-taking methods. These census coverage errors can take a variety of forms, including a person missed (an undercount), a person counted more than once (an overcount), or a person who should not have been counted, such as a child born after Census Day (another type of overcount). And because census data are central to so many critical functions, it is essential to assess census accuracy and improve the process when possible.

Statistical measurements of census coverage are obtained by comparing and matching the housing units and people counted by an independent sample or CCM survey to those counted by the census in and around the sample areas. The Bureau has developed separate address lists—one for the entire nation of over 134 million housing units that it is using to conduct the census and one for coverage-measurement sample areas—and is collecting each set of data through independent operations. The Bureau collected its CCM data from households in sample areas nationwide, as part of an operation that began in the middle of August and was completed in October 2010.

In our April 2010 report, we noted that in December 2009 the Bureau made numerous changes to the design of CCM that would reduce nonsampling error—such as human errors made when recording data during interviews—in CCM and its resulting estimates of census accuracy, thus providing census data users with more-reliable estimates.[17] These changes include increasing quality-assurance reinterviewing, hiring more CCM supervisors, and adding training for interviewers to improve interview techniques for local or other special situations (such as interviewing people who became homeless or have had to move frequently during the housing crisis). The December decision also reduced the CCM sample size by nearly 45 percent. The Bureau believes that this reduction will generate cost savings to pay for changes to reduce nonsampling error. We believe that, overall, these changes are reasonable efforts to improve survey quality. The Bureau's reduction in sample size will reduce precision of the estimates, yet the proposed changes should reduce nonsampling errors and thus provide users with more-reliable estimates.

Another challenge highlighted in our April 2010 report on CCM was determining the optimal time to collect data for some 170,000 housing units during person interviewing (PI), which began August 14 and ended October 16, 2010. The issue is that if the Bureau starts PI too early, it increases the chance that it overlaps with census data collection, possibly compromising the independence of the two different sets of data and introducing what is referred to as a "contamination bias" error into CCM data. However, if the Bureau starts PI too late, it increases the chance that respondents will not accurately remember household information from Census Day, introducing error (known as "recall bias") in the CCM count. In that report we recommended that the Bureau assess the trade-offs between starting early and introducing contamination bias or starting later and risking recall bias. The Bureau responded that it planned to study and measure some recall errors, but that there was no study planned to measure contamination bias in 2010 due to concerns with the possible contamination of census results in the study area. However, since both types of errors—contamination bias and recall bias— could affect the Bureau's conclusions about the accuracy of the census, it will be important for the Bureau to implement our recommendation and assess the trade-offs between the two types of biases in timing decisions. Moreover, this assessment could help the Bureau better inform the optimal timing for future census and coverage-measurement data collection operations.

FUNDAMENTAL REFORMS WILL BE NEEDED FOR A MORE COST-EFFECTIVE CENSUS IN 2020

While it will be important to assess and revamp existing census-taking activities, the results of prior enumerations underscore the fact that simply refining current methods—many of which have been in place for decades— will not bring about the reforms needed to control costs while maintaining accuracy given ongoing and newly emerging societal trends. Since 1970, the Bureau has used essentially the same approach to count the vast majority of the population. The Bureau develops an address list of the nation's housing units and mails census forms to each one for occupants to fill out and mail back. Over time, because of demographic and attitudinal trends, securing an acceptable response rate has become an increasing challenge, and the Bureau has spent more money with each census in order to secure a complete count. Indeed, the cost of conducting the census has, on average, doubled each decade since 1970, in constant 2010 dollars. If that rate of cost escalation continues into 2020, the nation could be facing a $30 billion census.

Despite the nation's greater investment in each census, the results are often no better than the previous decennial. For example, as noted earlier, while the unit cost of the census jumped from an average of around $70 in 2000 to around $98 in 2010, the mail response rate declined in 48 states. Our concerns about the rising cost and diminishing returns of the census are not new. In the mid-1990s, for example, we and others concluded that the established approach for taking the census in 1990 had exhausted its potential for counting the population cost-effectively and that fundamental design changes were needed to reduce census costs and improve the quality of data collected.[18]

A fundamental reexamination of the nation's approach to the census will require the Bureau to rethink its approach to planning, testing, implementing, monitoring, and evaluating the census, and addressing such questions as, why was a certain program initiated? What was the intended goal? Have significant changes occurred that affect its purpose? Does it use prevailing leading practices?

As one example, a critical factor affecting the cost of the census is the necessity for the Bureau to follow up on nonresponding housing units. The hourly wages of enumerators, their productivity, mileage reimbursement, and the need, in some cases, to return several times to an address to obtain a response can all drive up costs. Administrative records from other government agencies including driver licenses and school records can, if used in lieu of making multiple visits to a housing unit, significantly control costs. However, the Bureau would first need to resolve a number of questions including the quality and the coverage of the information supplied by the records and the policy and legal implications of accessing them.

On the basis of our earlier work on high-performing organizations, fundamental reforms will mean ensuring that the Bureau's organizational culture and structure, as well as its approach to strategic planning, human-capital management, internal collaboration, knowledge sharing, capital decision making, risk and change management, and other internal functions are aligned toward delivering more cost-effective outcomes.[19] Indeed, some of the operational problems that occurred during the 2010 and prior censuses are symptomatic of deeper organizational issues. For example, the lack of staff skilled in cost-estimation during the 2010 Census points to inadequate human-capital planning, while IT problems stemmed from not fully and consistently performing certain functions including IT investment management.

Going forward, it will be important for the Bureau, Congress, and other stakeholders to reach consensus on a number of reexamination areas, including the following, which have particular implications for controlling costs and improving accuracy:

- Which data collection approaches, the Internet and administrative records among them, have potential to improve data quality without compromising other Bureau goals and mandates such as confidentiality and timeliness?
- To what extent can private-sector and other sources of information such as maps, address lists, and geographic databases be employed to help support the census?
- How can the Bureau enhance how it partners with government and nongovernmental organizations, data users, grassroots organizations, and advisory groups to obtain their input and possibly better leverage their knowledge and services? What is the best way of maintaining congressional and stakeholder involvement and dialog throughout the course of the decade?
- What opportunities exist for the Bureau to leverage innovations in technology and social media to more fully engage census stakeholders and the general public throughout the decade on census issues, possibly identifying more cost-effective methods?
- To what extent can the Bureau use the American Community Survey—an ongoing Bureau survey of population and housing characteristics that is conducted throughout the decade—as a platform to test new census methods and systems?
- What are the implications of the Bureau's goal to conduct the 2020 Census at a lower cost than the 2010 Census on a cost per housing unit basis, adjusted for inflation? For example, how would this spending limit affect such considerations as accountability and data quality?
- How can the Bureau best balance the acquisition of advanced technology, some of which might not be fully mature until later in the decade, with the need to commit to particular systems sufficiently early in the decade to ensure the systems are fully tested and will work under census-like conditions?
- To what extent can the Bureau control costs and improve accuracy by targeting census-taking activities using local response rate and sociodemographic information from the 2010 Census, as well as other data sources and empirical evidence?

- What options exist for controlling the costs of particularly labor-intensive operations such as NRFU and building the Bureau's master address list without sacrificing accuracy?
- Can stakeholders reach agreement on a set of criteria that could be used to weigh the trade-offs associated with the need for high levels of accuracy on the one hand, and the increasing cost of achieving that accuracy on the other hand?

The Bureau, recognizing that it cannot afford to continue operating the way it does unless it fundamentally changes its method of doing business, has already taken some important first steps in addressing these questions as well as other areas. For example, the Bureau is looking to reform certain aspects of its IT systems planning, in part to ensure that the technical infrastructure needed for 2020 will be tested many times before operations begin. The Bureau is also rebuilding its research directorate to lead early planning efforts, and has plans to assess and monitor the skills and competencies needed for the 2020 headcount and evaluate the feasibility of administrative records.

Further, the Bureau has already developed a strategic plan for 2020 and other related documents that, among other things, lay out the structure of the Bureau's planning efforts; outline the Bureau's mission and vision for 2020 and the goals the Bureau seeks to meet to accomplish its mission; and describe the Bureau's plans for the research and testing phase of the next enumeration.

The Bureau's early planning efforts are noteworthy given the Bureau's long-standing challenges in this area. For example, in 1988, just prior to the 1990 Census, we noted that the Bureau's planning efforts generally started late, experienced delays, were incomplete, and failed to fully explore innovative approaches.[20] Planning for the 2000 Census also had its shortcomings. According to the Bureau, staff with little operational experience played key roles in the design process, which resulted in impractical reform ideas that could not be implemented. We also noted that the 2000 Census suffered from a persistent lack of priority-setting, coupled with minimal research, testing, and evaluation documentation to promote informed and timely decision making. And, while the planning process for the 2010 Census was initially more rigorous than for past decennials, in 2004 we reported that the Bureau's efforts lacked a substantial amount of supporting analysis, budgetary transparency, and other information, making it difficult for us, Congress, and other stakeholders to properly assess the feasibility of the Bureau's design and the extent to which it could lead to greater cost-effectiveness compared to alternative approaches.[21] As a result, in 2004, we recommended that the Bureau develop an operational plan for 2010 that consolidated budget, methodological, and other relevant information into a single, comprehensive document.

Although the Bureau later developed specific performance targets and an integrated project schedule for 2010, the other elements we recommended were only issued piecemeal, if available at all, and were never provided in a single, comprehensive document. Because this information was critical for facilitating a thorough, independent review of the Bureau's plans, as well as for demonstrating to Congress and other stakeholders that the Bureau could effectively design and manage operations and control costs, we believe that had it been available, it could have helped stave off, or at least reduce, the IT and other risks that confronted the Bureau as Census Day drew closer.

The Bureau's strategic plan for 2020, first issued in 2009, is a "living" document that will be updated as planning efforts progress. As the approach for 2020 takes shape, it will be important for the Bureau to avoid some of the problems it had in documenting the planning process for the 2010 Census, and pull all the planning elements together into a tactical plan or road map. This will help ensure the Bureau's reform initiatives stay on track, do not lose momentum, and coalesce into a viable path toward a more cost-effective 2020 Census. On the basis of our work on planning for the 2010 Census, a road map for 2020 could include, but not be limited to, the following elements that could be updated on a regular basis:

- specific, measurable performance goals, how the Bureau's efforts, procedures, and projects would contribute to those goals, and what performance measures would be used;
- descriptions of how the Bureau's approaches to human-capital management, organizational structure, IT acquisitions, and other internal functions are aligned with the performance goals;
- an assessment of the risks associated with each significant decennial operation, including the interrelationships between the operations and a description of relevant mitigation plans;
- detailed milestone estimates for each significant decennial operation, including estimated testing dates, and justification for any changes to milestone estimates;
- detailed life-cycle cost estimates of the decennial census that are credible, comprehensive, accurate, and well-documented as stipulated by Office of Management and Budget and GAO guidance; and

- a detailed description of all significant contracts the Bureau plans to enter into and a justification for the contracts.

A comprehensive road map could generate several important benefits. For example, it could help ensure a measure of transparency and facilitate a more collaborative approach to planning the next census. Specifically, an operational plan could function as a template for 2020 giving stakeholders a common framework to assess and comment on the design of the census and its supporting infrastructure, the resources needed to execute the design, and the extent to which it could lead to greater cost-effectiveness compared to alternative approaches. Further, it could be used to monitor the Bureau's progress in implementing its approach, and hold the agency accountable for results. Importantly, to the extent the plan—or aspects of it—are made available using social media tools, it could prompt greater and perhaps more constructive civic engagement on the census, by fostering an ongoing dialog involving individuals and communities of stakeholders throughout the decade. On December 8, 2010, the Senate approved a bill, the Census Oversight Efficiency and Management Reform Act of 2010.[22] If enacted, this bill, among its other provisions, would require the Director of the Census to submit an annual comprehensive status report on the next decennial census, beginning with the 2020 decennial census, to the appropriate congressional committees. The specific requirements in the bill for the annual plan include most of the elements discussed above.

Given the magnitude of the planning and transformation efforts facing the Bureau, another reexamination question is that of long-term stewardship governing the endeavor. Specifically, as the research, development, and testing efforts for 2020 will play out over the decade-long census life cycle, what is the optimal way to ensure continuity and accountability for an enterprise that takes years to complete and extends beyond the tenure of many elected political leaders?

Although the Director of the Census Bureau can, in concept, provide a measure of continuity, of the 11 census directors that have served since July 1969 (not including the current director), the average tenure was around 3 years, and only one director has served more than 5 years. Moreover, in the decade leading up to the 2010 Census, the Bureau was led by four different directors and several acting directors. The turnover in the Bureau's chief executive officer position makes it difficult to develop and sustain efforts that foster change, produce results, mitigate risks, and control costs over the long term.

Currently, census directors are nominated by the President with Senate confirmation. At the same time, the heads of a number of executive agencies serve fixed appointments, including the Director of the Office of Personnel Management (4 years), the Commissioner of Labor Statistics (4 years), and the Commissioner of Internal Revenue (5 years).

The census bill, recently passed by the Senate and discussed above, includes a provision for a 5-year tenure for the Census Director. We believe that the continuity resulting from a fixed-term appointment could provide the following benefits to the Bureau:

- Strategic vision. The Director needs to build a long-term vision for the Bureau that extends beyond the current decennial census. Strategic planning, human-capital succession planning, and life-cycle cost estimates for the Bureau all span the decade.
- Sustaining stakeholder relationships. The Director needs to continually expand and develop working relationships and partnerships with governmental, political, and other professional officials in both the public and private sectors to obtain their input, support, and participation in the Bureau's activities.
- Accountability. The life-cycle cost for a decennial census spans a decade, and decisions made early in the decade about the next decennial census guide the research, investments, and tests carried out throughout the entire 10-year period. Institutionalizing accountability over an extended period may help long-term decennial initiatives provide meaningful and sustainable results.

Overall, the obstacles to conducting a cost-effective census have grown with each decade, and as the Bureau looks toward the next enumeration, it might confront its biggest challenge to date. As the Bureau's past experience has shown, early investments in planning can help reduce the costs and risks of its downstream operations. Therefore, while Census Day 2020 is 10 years away, it is not too early for stakeholders to start considering the reforms needed to help ensure the next headcount is as cost-effective as possible.

CONCLUSIONS

Although the complete results of the 2010 Census are still some years away, several preliminary lessons learned for the next enumeration have already begun to emerge. They include the benefits of a replacement questionnaire, the removal of late mail returns from the NRFU workload, and hiring locally. Focus areas for improvement include revisiting the Bureau's staffing model, ensuring the Bureau emphasizes quality as well as production during NRFU, better IT management, and ensuring a high-quality address file is used to carry out VDC operations.

That said, perhaps the most important lesson learned comes from the collective experience gained from the 1990, 2000, and now 2010 enumerations: the Bureau goes to great lengths each decade to improvespecific census-taking activities, but these incremental modifications have not kept pace with societal changes that make the population increasingly difficult to locate and count cost-effectively. Therefore, as the Bureau looks toward 2020, it will be important for it to reexamine both the fundamental design of the enumeration, as well as its management and culture to ensure that the Bureau's business practices and systems enhance its capacity to conduct an accurate count, control costs, manage risks, and be more nimble in adapting to social, demographic, technological, and other changes that can be expected in the years ahead.

The Bureau is taking some initial steps toward rethinking the census. At the same time, past experience has shown that the Bureau cannot plan and execute a successful enumeration on its own. Indeed, the noteworthy achievements of the 2010 Census occurred because of the shared efforts of the Bureau, and its parent organizations the Department of Commerce and the Economics and Statistics Administration, Congress, and thousands of other parties. It will be important for these and additional stakeholders to maintain their focus on the census throughout the decade in order to achieve desired results. Certain census reforms could require legislative changes, and any new procedures will need to be thoroughly vetted, tested, and refined. Although the next enumeration is 10 years away, the groundwork for building a new census infrastructure is already under way. The bottom line is that while the urgency of the 2010 Census has subsided, it is by no means any less important to the nation.

RECOMMENDATIONS FOR EXECUTIVE ACTION

As the Bureau plans for the next decennial census in 2020, in order to support efforts to reexamine the fundamental design of the decennial census, and help refine existing operations should they be used again in the 2020

Census, we recommend that the Secretary of Commerce direct the Under Secretary of the Economics and Statistics Administration, as well as the Census Director, to take the following six actions:

- To help enhance the Bureau's performance and accountability, improve the transparency of the planning process, gauge whether the Bureau is on-track toward a more cost-effective 2020 Census, and foster greater public dialog about the census, the Bureau should develop an operational plan or road map for 2020 that integrates performance, budget, methodological, schedule, and other information that would be updated as needed and posted on the Bureau's Web site and other social media outlets, and develop a mechanism that allows for and harnesses input from census stakeholders and individuals.
- To refine its approach to recruiting, the Bureau should evaluate current economic factors that are associated with and predictive of employee interest in census work, such as national and regional unemployment levels, and use these available data to determine the potential temporary workforce pool and adjust its recruiting approach.
- To help ensure that the Bureau's procedures for NRFU result in the collection of high-quality data, the Bureau's procedures for the timely completion of NRFU should emphasize the collection of high-quality data and proper enumeration techniques as much as speed.
- To improve the fingerprinting process of temporary workers, the Bureau should revise or modify training so that field staff are provided with numerous practice opportunities for collecting fingerprints prior to each operation.
- To ensure that the Bureau improves its ability to manage future IT acquisitions, the Bureau should immediately establish and enforce a system-acquisition management policy that incorporates best practices in system- and software-acquisition management.
- To help ensure the Bureau compiles an accurate address list for VDC operations in 2020, the Bureau should research how duplicate addresses were inadvertently included in the VDC workload.

AGENCY COMMENTS AND OUR EVALUATION

The Secretary of Commerce provided written comments on a draft of this report on December 7, 2010. The comments are reprinted in appendix II. The

Department of Commerce generally agreed with the overall findings and recommendations of the report. In addition, the Secretary of Commerce provided the Bureau's technical comments and suggestions where additional context might be needed, and we revised the report to reflect these comments where appropriate.

The Bureau noted that our report did not acknowledge the steps it took to modify its recruiting plans prior to NRFU. However, we do discuss the Bureau's modifications to its recruiting plans. Specifically, we stated that "once the Bureau had an adequate pool of candidates for 2010, it attempted to limit the number of additional applicants, taking such steps as discontinuing the advertising of census jobs in mailed out census materials."

The Bureau also commented that it wanted to discuss our analysis that found that the fast pace of NRFU was associated with the collection of less-complete household data, noting that its own analysis of a similar question did not yield the same finding. On December 7, 2010, we met with Bureau staff to discuss the methodologies and variables used in each analysis. After discussing our methodology and results, Bureau staff explained that their analysis was preliminary and not as comprehensive as our analysis. Further, they acknowledged that they used a different methodology and different variables.

The Bureau, in commenting on our finding related to fingerprinting temporary workers, noted that it was unclear as to ways in which extending training, which usually requires spending more time and money, would streamline fingerprinting efforts. To clarify this section we changed the body of the report. The text now reads, "In looking forward to 2020, the Bureau should revise or modify training so that field staff are provided with numerous practice opportunities for collecting fingerprints prior to each operation."

Robert Goldenkoff
Director
Strategic Issues

APPENDIX I: OBJECTIVES, SCOPE, AND METHODOLOGY

The objectives of this report were to assess the implementation of (1) nonresponse follow-up (NRFU), the largest and most costly census field operation, where the U.S. Census Bureau (Bureau) sends enumerators to collect data from households that did not mail back their census forms, and (2) other key follow-up field operations that were critical for ensuring a complete count; and (3) identify key questions and focus areas that will be important for the Bureau, Congress, and census stakeholders to consider going forward now that planning for the next enumeration is underway.

To meet our objectives, we used a combination of approaches and methods to examine the conduct of these operations. These included statistical analyses; surveys of the Bureau's 494 local census office (LCO) managers; analysis of mail response and form check-in rates from Bureau cost and progress systems; interviews with key bureau headquarters officials and LCO managers and staff; observation of LCO's NRFU operations; and reviews of relevant documentation including our prior work on the planning and implementation of the 1990, 2000, and 2010 Censuses.

To examine the factors that affected the implementation of NRFU and vacant/delete check operations (VDC), we interviewed LCO managers and other supervisory staff and observed operations at 28 LCOs we visited across the country. We selected LCOs because they were located in hardto-count areas as determined by data from the 2000 Census. To make these selections, we also used other factors such as their percentage of rural population to obtain diversity in urban/rural populations, and proximity to hurricane-affected areas. Selections for VDC observations were based primarily on locations with high rates of vacant and delete classifications, and they were chosen to include a mix of urban, suburban, and rural LCO located in all regions of the country. (See below for a complete list of the offices we visited.) During these visits, which took place from April to July 2010, we observed office operations to see how office staff were processing questionnaires using the Paper-Based Operations Control System (PBOCS) and capturing fingerprints with live scanners, attended enumerator training, and observed enumerators in the field go door-to-door to collect census data for NRFU, NRFU reinterview, and VDC. Because offices were judgmentally selected, our findings from these visits cannot be projected to the universe of LCOs.

To obtain a national perspective on the conduct of NRFU and other field data collection operations, we conducted a panel survey of all 494 LCO managers from March to August 2010 using six questionnaires. The survey was designed to examine (1) factors that affect the cost and performance of local data collection efforts, and (2) LCO managers' satisfaction with information technology (IT) systems and other management support functions. Response rate was at least 75 percent for each survey questionnaire.

The practical difficulties of developing and administering a survey may introduce errors—from how a particular question is interpreted, for example, or from differences in the sources of information available to respondents when answering a question. Therefore, we included steps in developing and administering the questionnaire to minimize such errors. For instance, we conducted pretests to check that (1) the questions were clear and unambiguous, (2) terminology was used correctly, (3) the questionnaire did not place an undue burden on agency officials, (4) the information could feasibly be obtained, and (5) the survey was comprehensive and unbiased. Pretest sites were selected for each wave to emphasize variation among urban and rural LCOs. Pretests were conducted over the phone, mostly as cognitive pretests in which the respondent completed the survey during the pretest. We made changes to the content and format of the questionnaire after review by a GAO survey expert and after each of the pretests, based on the feedback we received.

To examine whether the pace of NRFU was associated with the collection of less-complete data, in addition to the efforts described above, we analyzed Bureau proxy and closeout rates, and the time it took for an LCO to complete the NRFU workload. In order to determine whether the durations of 2010 NRFU production activities were associated with lower-quality work, we conducted regression analyses using data from the Bureau's Cost and Progress System, PBOCS, and Matching Review and Coding System (MaRCS). These analyses assessed whether indicators of lower-quality enumeration such as the collection of proxy data from a neighbor and closeout interviews, where a housing unit is occupied but no interview was obtained, were associated with the number of days that the LCO spent conducting NRFU production activities, after adjusting for other factors associated with the timeliness of completion and workload. We used two regression models: one model tested the association between the number of days it took each LCO to complete 100 percent of its workload and quality factors; the other regression model tested the association between quick completion and quality factors. We also analyzed cost data weekly for both NRFU and VDC to determine whether those operations were within their respective budgets.

To assess the reliability of the data, we reviewed Bureau electronic documentation to gain information about the data and their sources. We examined data from the Bureau's Cost and Progress, PBOCS, and MaRCS systems to check for logical errors and inconsistencies, and followed up with agency officials knowledgeable about the data in cases where we had questions about potential errors or inconsistencies, and to inquire about the accuracy and completeness of the entry and processing of the data. Values are updated by the Bureau throughout the operations, and may be revised by the

Bureau even after the operations close. On the basis of our efforts, we determined that the data were sufficiently reliable for the purposes of this engagement.

Finally, to identify preliminary steps the Bureau can take to help transform its management and culture, we reviewed our prior work on governmentwide reexamination, as well as leading practices and attributes in the areas of IT management, organizational performance, collaboration, stewardship, and human capital. In addition, we reviewed census planning material, prior GAO work on census planning and development efforts, and spoke with Bureau officials about their needs and plans for management and cultural transformation.

We conducted this performance audit from December 2009 until December 2010 in accordance with generally accepted government auditing standards. Those standards require that we plan and perform the audits to obtain sufficient, appropriate evidence to provide a reasonable basis for our findings and conclusions based on our audit objectives. We believe that the evidence obtained provides a reasonable basis for our findings and conclusions based on our audit objectives.

LOCAL CENSUS OFFICES VISITED IN THIS REVIEW

Tucson, Arizona
Fresno and San Francisco, California
New Castle, Delaware
Fort Myers, Florida Atlanta, Georgia
Chicago (2 locations), Illinois
New Orleans, Louisiana
Baltimore and Seat Pleasant, Maryland
Boston, Massachusetts
Detroit, Michigan Meridian, Mississippi
Cape Girardeau and St. Louis, Missouri
Las Vegas (2 locations), Nevada
Albuquerque, New Mexico
Bronx, Brooklyn, and Manhattan, New York
Asheville and Fayetteville, North Carolina
Philadelphia, Pennsylvania
Dallas and Houston, Texas
Washington, District of Columbia

APPENDIX II: COMMENTS FROM THE DEPARTMENT OF COMMERCE

December 7, 2010

Mr. Robert Goldenkoff
Director
Strategic Issues
U.S. Government Accountability Office
Washington, DC 20548

Dear Mr. Goldenkoff:

The Department of Commerce appreciates the opportunity to comment on the U.S. Government Accountability Office's draft report entitled "2010 Census: Data Collection Operations Were Generally Completed as Planned, But Longstanding Challenges Suggest Need for Fundamental Reforms" (GAO-11-193). The Department of Commerce's comments on this report are enclosed.

Sincerely,

Gary Locke

Enclosure

Department of Commerce
Comments on the
United States Government Accountability Office
Draft Report Entitled "2010 Census: Data Collection Operations Were Generally Completed as Planned, But Longstanding Challenges Suggest Need for Fundamental Reforms"

(GAO-11-193)
December 2010

The Department of Commerce (Department) would like to thank the U.S. Government Accountability Office (GAO) for its efforts in examining the 2010 Census Nonresponse Followup (NRFU) and other field operations to seek out improved approaches to securing greater participation from the public and to reduce extensive operating costs in the next census.

The Department generally agrees with the overall findings and with the recommendations regarding items suggested for study for conducting the 2020 Census. The Census Bureau does, however, wish to provide a few comments about the statements and conclusions in this report:

- Page 13, second paragraph: "With respect to staffing levels, the Bureau set a recruitment goal of nearly 3.7 million qualified applicants and achieved 104 percent of this goal..."

  Response: As clarification, the Census Bureau notes that our goal was 3.8 million total applicants, in order to yield a sufficient number of qualified applicants. Not all applicants we recruit qualify for census work. In Census 2000, only about 73 percent of the applicants ended up being qualified. For the 2010 Census, this figure was about 77 percent. This comment also applies to a similar statement on page 3 of the report.

- Page 13, last paragraph: "According to the Bureau, based on past experience, it set its recruiting goal at five times the number of persons .... develop more accurate recruiting targets. It will also be important for the Bureau to adhere to recruiting goals so that additional costs are not incurred."

  Response: The Census Bureau agrees that initial plans for 2010 Census recruiting were driven by its Census 2000 experience; however, this section of the report does not acknowledge that, based on the state of the economy in late 2009 and early 2010, the Census Bureau took several steps to modify its recruiting plans prior to the peak recruiting for 2010 field operations, such as NRFU. The Census Bureau certainly agrees that monitoring economic conditions closely to develop and implement a recruiting strategy for the 2020 Census is important.

- Page 16, first paragraph: "...if an enumerator was unable to collect data from either the household or a proxy respondent a "closeout interview" was used where household information was later determined using statistical methods based on neighborhood characteristics."

  and

  Page 19, first paragraph: "... a closeout interview is one where no interview is conducted and household information is later determined using statistical methods."

  Response: The Census Bureau recommends some slight revisions to these sentences. As currently written, these statements might be read to imply that field staff was responsible for determining household characteristics based on the characteristics of neighboring units. Explaining that this imputation step takes place at headquarters during data processing would provide clarity and additional accuracy. Also, a statement that implies that no data are collected during a closeout interview is not correct. Field staff sometimes obtained a population count directly from a resident.

- Page 18, last paragraph: "Significantly, our analysis of Bureau data found that the fast pace of NRFU was associated with the collection of less complete household data."

  Response: The Census Bureau would be interested in discussing these findings in more detail, because its analysis of a similar question did not yield the same finding.

- Page 24, lines 16-17: "In looking forward to 2020, the Bureau could streamline fingerprint taking by extending training sessions to allot more time for the process."

  Response: The Census Bureau would appreciate additional clarity regarding this recommendation. The Census Bureau is unclear as to ways in which extending training, which usually requires spending more time and money, would streamline fingerprinting efforts.

- Page 47, second paragraph: "...the noteworthy achievements of the 2010 Census occurred because of the shared efforts of the Bureau, Congress and thousands of other parties."

  Response: This sentence should specifically include the Department of Commerce and the Economics and Statistics Administration (ESA). Particularly in 2009 and 2010, ESA played a significant role in helping to make the 2010 Census a success.

- Page 48, second paragraph: "...we recommend that the Secretary of Commerce direct the Census Director to take the following six actions:..."

  Response: The Secretary of Commerce should direct the Under Secretary of the Economics and Statistics Administration (ESA) as well as the Census Director. ESA has

    management oversight responsibility of the Census Bureau and has been actively engaged in planning for the 2020 Census, including development of effective, efficient, and forward thinking integrated management approaches and systems that will result in successful and cost-effective operations across the bureau's programs and activities.

    - Page 50, second paragraph: "We are sending copies of this report to the Secretary of Commerce, the Director of the U.S. Census Bureau, and interested congressional committees."

      Response: Please also send a copy of the report to the Under Secretary for Economic Affairs (ESA).

In conclusion, we want to acknowledge the GAO's extensive work in reviewing these activities, and appreciate its ongoing efforts to help us develop a successful evaluation plan for the 2020 Census.

Note: Page numbers in the draft report may differ from those in this report.

End Notes

[1] 13 U.S.C. § 141(b).

[2] See for example: GAO, *Decennial Census: Preliminary 1990 Lessons Learned Indicate Need to Rethink Census Approach*, GAO/T-GGD-90-18 (Washington, D.C.: Aug. 8, 1990); and *2000 Census: Progress Made on Design, but Risks Remain*, GAO/GGD-97-142 (Washington, D.C.: July 14, 1997).

[3] GAO, *2010 Census: Key Efforts to Include Hard-to-Count Populations Went Generally as Planned; Improvements Could Make the Efforts More Effective for Next Census*, GAO-11-45 (Washington, D.C.: Dec. 14, 2010); and *2010 Census: Follow-up Should Reduce Coverage Errors, but Effects on Demographic Groups Need to Be Determined*, GAO-11-154 (Washington, D.C.: Dec. 14, 2010).

[4] See for example: GAO, *Information Technology Investment Management: A Framework for Assessing and Improving Process Maturity*, GAO-04-394G (Washington, D.C.: March 2004); *Human Capital: Key Principles for Effective Strategic Workforce Planning*, GAO-04-39 (Washington, D.C.: Dec. 11, 2003); *Comptroller General's Forum, High-Performing Organizations: Metrics, Means, and Mechanisms for Achieving High Performance in the 21st Century Public Management Environment*, GAO-04-343SP (Washington, D.C.: Feb. 13, 2004); *21st Century Challenges: Reexamining the Base of the Federal Government*, GAO-05-325SP (Washington, D.C.: February 2005); and *Results-Oriented Government: Practices That Can Help Enhance and Sustain Collaboration among Federal Agencies*, GAO-06-15 (Washington, D.C.: Oct. 21, 2005).

[5] High-risk areas are areas GAO has called special attention to because of their vulnerability to mismanagement or their broad need for reform. GAO, *Information Technology: Significant Problems of Critical Automation Program Contribute to Risks Facing 2010 Census*, GAO-08-550T (Washington, D.C.: Mar. 5, 2008).

[6] GAO-04-343SP.

[7] In the 2000 Census, the Bureau mailed out both long- and short-form questionnaires. The short-form questionnaire had a higher response rate because it had fewer questions. For the 2010 Census, the Bureau used only a short-form questionnaire. For this report we use the 2000 Census short-form mail response rate when comparing 2000 and 2010 mail-back response rates.

[8] GAO, *2010 Census: Census Bureau Should Take Action to Improve the Credibility and Accuracy of Its Cost Estimate for the Decennial Census*, GAO-08-554 (Washington, D.C.: June 16, 2008).

[9] In order to determine whether the pace of the 2010 Census NRFU was associated with lower-quality work, we conducted regression analysis using Census data to assess whether indicators of lower-quality work were associated with NRFU completion time among the 494 LCOs after adjusting for other factors associated with the timeliness of completion and workload.

[10] The National Crime Prevention and Privacy Compact, enacted in 1998, generally requires that fingerprints be submitted with all requests for criminal history record checks for noncriminal justice purposes; 42 U.S.C. § 14616. For the 2000 Census, the Federal Bureau of Investigation (FBI) did not have the capacity to timely process the fingerprints of the Census's temporary workforce, so employees were subject to only a name background check.

[11] A well-defined enterprise architecture provides a clear and comprehensive picture of an entity, whether it is an organization (e.g., a federal department) or a functional or mission area that

cuts across more than one organization (e.g., personnel management). This picture consists of snapshots of both the enterprise's current or "As Is" environment and its target or "To Be" environment, as well as a capital-investment road map for transitioning from the current to the target environment.

[12] GAO, *Information Technology Management: Census Bureau Has Implemented Many Key Practices, but Additional Actions Are Needed*, GAO-05-661 (Washington, D.C.: June 16, 2005).

[13] GAO, *Census 2010: Census at Critical Juncture for Implementing Risk Reduction Strategies*, GAO-08-659T (Washington, D.C.: Apr. 9, 2008); *Information Technology: Census Bureau Needs to Improve Its Risk Management of Decennial Systems*, GAO-08-259T (Washington, D.C.: Dec. 11, 2007); and GAO-08-550T.

[14] GAO, *2010 Census: Data Collection Is Under Way, but Reliability of Key Information Technology Systems Remains a Risk*, GAO-10-567T (Washington, D.C.: Mar. 25, 2010); *2010 Census: Key Enumeration Activities Are Moving Forward, but Information Technology Systems Remain a Concern*, GAO-10-430T (Washington, D.C.: Feb. 23, 2010); and *2010 Census: Census Bureau Continues to Make Progress in Mitigating Risks to a Successful Enumeration, but Still Faces Various Challenges*, GAO-10-132T (Washington, D.C.: Oct. 7, 2009).

[15] See for example: GAO-05-661; GAO, *Census Bureau: Important Activities for Improving Management of Key 2010 Decennial Acquisitions Remain to be Done*, GAO-06-444T (Washington, D.C.: Mar. 1, 2006); *Information Technology: Census Bureau Needs to Improve Its Risk Management of Decennial Systems*, GAO-08-79 (Washington, D.C.: Oct. 5, 2007); and *Information Technology: Census Bureau Testing of 2010 Decennial Systems Can Be Strengthened*, GAO-09-262 (Washington, D.C.: Mar. 5, 2009).

[16] GAO-08-554.

[17] GAO, *2010 Census: Plans for Census Coverage Measurement Are on Track, but Additional Steps Will Improve Its Usefulness*, GAO-10-324 (Washington, D.C.: Apr. 23, 2010).

[18] GAO/GGD-97-142.

[19] See for example: GAO-04-394G, GAO-04-39, GAO-04-343SP, GAO-05-325SP, and GAO-06-15.

[20] GAO, *Transition Series: Commerce Issues*, OCG-89-11TR (Washington, D.C.: Nov. 1, 1988).

[21] GAO, *2010 Census: Cost and Design Issues Need to Be Addressed Soon*, GAO-04-37 (Washington, D.C.: Jan. 15, 2004).

[22] S. 3167, 111th Cong. § 2 (2010).

In: The 2010 Census: Operations and Outcomes   ISBN: 978-1-61324-348-0
Editors: K. De Luca and C. Moretti   © 2011 Nova Science Publishers, Inc.

Chapter 3

2010 CENSUS: KEY EFFORTS TO INCLUDE HARD-TO-COUNT POPULATIONS WENT GENERALLY AS PLANNED; IMPROVEMENTS COULD MAKE THE EFFORTS MORE EFFECTIVE FOR NEXT CENSUS[*]

United States Government Accountability Office

WHY GAO DID THIS STUDY

To overcome the long-standing challenge of enumerating hard-tocount (HTC) groups such as minorities and renters, the U.S. Census Bureau (Bureau), used outreach programs, such as paid advertising, and partnered with thousands of organizations to enlist their support for the census. The Bureau also conducted Service-Based Enumeration (SBE), which was designed to count people who frequent soup kitchens or other service providers, and the Be Counted/Questionnaire Assistance Center (QAC) program, designed to count individuals who believed the census had missed them. As requested, GAO assessed how the design of these efforts compared to 2000 and the extent to which they were implemented as planned. GAO

---

[*] This is an edited, reformatted and augmented version of United States Government Accountability Office publication GAO-11-45, dated December 2010.

reviewed Bureau budget, planning, operational, and evaluation documents; observed enumeration efforts in 12 HTC areas; surveyed local census office managers; and interviewed Bureau officials.

WHAT GAO RECOMMENDS

GAO recommends that the Bureau take steps to improve the effectiveness of its outreach and enumeration activities aimed at HTC groups, including developing a predictive model to better allocate paid advertising funds, improving coordination between partnership and local census staff, revisiting SBE staffing guidance, and ensuring Be Counted/QAC sites are more visible and optimally located. Commerce generally agreed with the overall findings and recommendations.

WHAT GAO FOUND

The Bureau better positioned itself to reach out to and enumerate HTC populations in 2010 in part by addressing a number of key challenges from 2000. The Bureau's outreach efforts were generally more robust compared to 2000. For example, compared to 2000, the Bureau used more reliable data to target advertising; focused a larger share of its advertising dollars on HTC groups, such as non-English-speaking audiences; and strengthened its monitoring abilities so that the Bureau was able to run additional advertising in locations where mail response rates were lagging. The Bureau also significantly expanded the partnership program by hiring about 2,800 partnership staff in 2010 compared to around 600 in 2000. As a result, staff were not spread as thin. The number of languages they spoke increased from 35 in 2000 to 145 for the 2010 Census.

Despite these enhancements, the outreach efforts still faced challenges. For example, while most of the partnership staff GAO interviewed reported having mutually supportive relationships with local census offices, about half of the local census office managers surveyed were dissatisfied with the level of coordination, noting duplication of effort in some cases. Additionally, a tracking database that partnership staff were to use to help manage their efforts was not user-friendly nor was it kept current.

The Bureau also improved the key enumeration programs aimed at HTC groups and the efforts were generally implemented as planned, but additional refinements could improve them for 2020. For example, the Bureau expanded SBE training by teaching staff how to enumerate all types of SBE facilities, which gave the Bureau more flexibility in scheduling enumerations, and advance visits helped enhance service providers' readiness for the enumeration. Nevertheless, while most local census office managers were satisfied with SBE staffing levels, pockets of dissatisfaction existed and observers noted what appeared to be a surplus of enumerators with little work to do in some locations. While overstaffing can lead to unnecessarily higher labor costs, understaffing can also be problematic because it can affect the accuracy of the overall count, and it will be important for the Bureau to review the results of SBE to staff SBE efficiently in 2020.

For the Be Counted/QAC program, the Bureau addressed visibility and site selection challenges from 2000 by developing banners to prominently display site locations and hours of operation and updating site selection guidance. For 2010, the Bureau opened around 38,000 sites and completed the monthlong operation under budget. However, the Bureau experienced recurring challenges with ensuring that the sites were visible from street level and were in areas with potential for high levels of activity, and the overall effort was resource intensive relative to the average of 20 forms that were returned and checked in from each site. Moving forward, it will be important for the Bureau to explore ways to maximize the program's ability to increase the number of forms checked in for 2020.

December 14, 2010
The Honorable Thomas R. Carper
Chairman

The Honorable John McCain
Ranking Member
Subcommittee on Federal Financial Management, Government Information, Federal Services, and International Security
Committee on Homeland Security and Governmental Affairs
United States Senate

The Honorable Darrell E. Issa
Ranking Member
Committee on Oversight and Government Reform

House of Representatives

The Honorable William Lacy Clay
Chairman
The Honorable Patrick T. McHenry
Ranking Member
Subcommittee on Information Policy, Census, and National Archives
Committee on Oversight and Government Reform
House of Representatives

A complete and accurate census is becoming an increasingly daunting task, in part because the nation's population is growing larger, more diverse, and more reluctant to participate. When the census misses a person who should have been included, it results in an undercount; an overcount occurs when an individual is counted more than once. Such errors are particularly problematic because of their differential impact on various subgroups. Minorities, renters, and children, for example, are more likely to be undercounted by the census while more affluent groups, such as people with vacation homes, are more likely to be enumerated more than once. As census data are used to apportion seats in Congress, redraw congressional districts, and allocate billions of dollars in federal assistance to states and local governments, improving coverage and reducing the differential undercount[1] are critical.

To help reduce the undercount for the 2010 Census, the U.S. Census Bureau (Bureau) embarked on a number of outreach and enumeration activities aimed at getting the hard-to-count (HTC) populations to participate in the census. On the outreach side, the Bureau implemented a communications campaign that included paid media and partnership activities (among others) to target advertisements and engage government and community organizations in support of the census. On the enumeration side, the Bureau relied on such efforts as Service-Based Enumeration (SBE) to enumerate individuals residing in less conventional housing, such as shelters and tent encampments, and the Be Counted/Questionnaire Assistance Centers (QAC) programs to count people who believed they did not receive a census form.

One key to a successful census is a high mail participation rate, which helps the Bureau obtain more accurate data and reduce costs. The mail participation rate—which the Bureau defines as the percentage of forms mailed back by households that received them—was 74 percent for 2010, the same as in 2000.[2] Considering the nation's diversity and other sociodemographic trends that adversely affect participation rates, this was an important accomplishment.

Because of your interest in the Bureau's efforts to boost census participation and reduce the differential undercount, we reviewed the design and implementation of key outreach and enumeration programs aimed at HTC populations. In so doing, we paid particular attention to assessing (1) how the design of these programs compared to 2000 and (2) the extent to which the Bureau implemented these programs as planned and where refinements might be needed should these efforts be used in the 2020 Census.

This report is one of three we are releasing today.[3] Of the other two, one assesses the implementation of key field data collection operations, and the other examines the implementation of operations aimed at reducing census coverage errors. Both reports identify preliminary lessons learned, as well as potential focus areas for improvement for the 2020 Census.

To assess how the Bureau's efforts to reach out to and enumerate HTC populations compared to 2000, we reviewed and analyzed budget, planning, operational, and evaluative data and documents for the 2000 and 2010 paid media, partnership, SBE, and Be Counted/QAC activities. We chose these activities because they constitute the majority of the budget for outreach efforts or, according to the Bureau, were enumeration activities that contributed to reducing the differential undercount in 2000. For example, paid advertising accounted for approximately 39 percent ($258,738,551) of the Bureau's originally planned $660 million communication campaign effort, and the partnership program accounted for over 56 percent ($364,331,089) of the campaign.[4] According to the Bureau, the Be Counted/QAC program was an important part of the Bureau's efforts to enumerate people often missed by the census, including people who had no usual residence on Census Day, such as transients, migrants, or seasonal farm workers. In addition, we attended presentations on the paid media program by the Bureau and its contractor, DraftFCB, which assisted the Bureau with creating promotional campaigns to research, develop, and target the paid advertising efforts. We also reviewed Bureau, Department of Commerce Inspector General, and our reports on the 2010 and 2000 censuses, and interviewed cognizant Bureau officials at headquarters and local census offices.

To evaluate whether implementation proceeded as planned and identify areas for improvement in 2020, we conducted 78 observations of enumerators as they visited SBE facilities, including 22 targeted non-sheltered outdoor locations (TNSOL)—such as parks and under bridges where people experiencing homelessness were sometimes counted. We interviewed enumerators in 12 urban local census offices across the country, such as those in Boston, Chicago, Dallas, and Los Angeles, and interviewed enumerators' supervisors, known as crew leaders, in some of the local census offices we visited.[5] Further, we conducted observations of 51 Be Counted/QAC sites in 12 urban areas. For the SBE and Be Counted/QAC observations, we selected offices located in HTC areas as determined by data from the 2000 Census. While these sites were not selected randomly, we considered factors such as ethnic and geographic diversity in selecting them.

To gain greater insight on the partnership program, we interviewed 11 partnership staff who represented historically HTC populations and different ethnic groups in the Bureau's Atlanta, Charlotte, Philadelphia, and Los Angeles regions. We selected these regions based on, in part, the allocation of partnership staff, but the sites were not randomly selected and results cannot be generalized nationwide.

To obtain information on the local implementation of the Bureau's outreach and enumeration efforts, we surveyed the Bureau's entire population of 494 local census office managers (LCOM) using a series of online questionnaires about their experience in managing local census office activities and enumeration efforts. The surveys were conducted in six waves from March through September 2010. Each survey had a response rate of at least 70 percent and was thus sufficiently reliable for providing evidence to support our findings, conclusions, and recommendations.

We analyzed Bureau data on the distribution of Be Counted/QAC sites among HTC census tracts and local census offices. We analyzed cost and progress data for SBE and Be Counted/QACs and analyzed data on partnership and Be Counted/QAC activities from the automated system the Bureau used to track its partnership contacts, the Integrated Partnership Contact Database.[6] To further identify and assess the Bureau's outreach and enumeration efforts for HTC populations, we interviewed Bureau officials to obtain additional details about paid media, partnerships, SBE, and Be Counted/QAC.

This report is part of our larger review of lessons learned from the 2010 Census that can help inform the Bureau's planning efforts for 2020. The Bureau is also evaluating its efforts to reach out to and enumerate HTC populations and plans to issue the results by December 2012.

We conducted this performance audit from January 2010 to December 2010 in accordance with generally accepted government auditing standards. Those standards require that we plan and perform the audit to obtain sufficient, appropriate evidence to provide a reasonable basis for our findings and conclusions based on our audit objectives. We believe that the evidence obtained provides a reasonable basis for our findings and conclusions based on our audit objectives.

On December 8, 2010, the Secretary of Commerce provided written comments on the draft report, which are reprinted in appendix I. The Department of Commerce generally agreed with the overall findings and recommendations of the report.

BACKGROUND

To improve participation in the census among HTC groups as well as the general population, the Bureau implemented a number of outreach and enumeration activities from January 2008 through September 2010. In this report, we focus on the following four efforts:

- paid media
- partnerships
- SBE, and
- Be Counted/QAC

The four components of the outreach efforts, known collectively as the Integrated Communications Campaign, were paid media, a partnership program, public relations and an educational program called Census in Schools. According to Bureau officials, the components were designed to work together to unify census messages and communicate them to diverse audiences via various outlets in order to improve mail response and reduce the differential undercount. An appropriation in the American Recovery and Reinvestment Act of 2009 (Recovery Act) allowed the Bureau to increase the communications campaign's initial budget of $410 million by an additional $220 million.[7]

The Bureau's regional census centers (RCC) were responsible for administering the partnership program, with partnership coordinators and team leaders at each RCC overseeing the work of the partnership specialists and partnership assistants. Local census offices played a more limited role in outreach efforts, and while the local census offices reported to RCCs, they had a different reporting structure than the partnership program.

SBE was meant to help ensure that people without conventional housing were included in the count. From March 28 through March 30, 2010, the Bureau attempted to enumerate those without conventional housing at facilities where they received services or at outdoor locations, such as parked cars, tent encampments, and on the street. The Bureau developed a list of potential outdoor locations based on several sources, including 2000 Census data and input from community leaders.

The Bureau's Be Counted program, which ran from March 19 to April 19, 2010, was designed to reach those who may not have received a census questionnaire, including people who did not have a usual residence on April 1, 2010, such as transients, migrants, and seasonal farm workers.[8] The program made questionnaires available at community centers, libraries, places of worship, and other public locations throughout the country. Individuals were to pick up the forms from these sites and mail the completed questionnaires to the Bureau. Some of the sites also included a staffed QAC to help people, especially those with limited English proficiency, complete their questionnaires.

THE BUREAU'S OUTREACH AND PROMOTION EFFORTS WERE GENERALLY MORE ROBUST COMPARED TO THOSE IN 2000 AND WERE IMPLEMENTED AS PLANNED, BUT THEY COULD BE FURTHER IMPROVED

Paid Media Plans Built in Better Targeting

The Bureau refined its paid media efforts for 2010, in part to address challenges from the 2000 Census. For example, in 2000, to target advertising to certain population groups and areas, the Bureau used data on measures of civic participation, such as voting in elections. However, the Bureau noted that civic participation did not appear to be a primary indicator of an individual's willingness to participate in the census. To better motivate participation among different population groups, for 2010 the Bureau used, among other data sources, actual participation data from the 2000 Census, as well as market and attitudinal research that identified five mindsets people have about the census. These mindsets ranged from the "leading edge" (those who are highly likely to participate) to the "cynical fifth" (those who are less likely to participate because they doubt the census provides tangible benefits and are concerned that the census is an invasion of privacy and that the information collected will be misused). The Bureau used this information to tailor its paid media efforts. Moreover, in 2000 the Bureau did not buy additional paid media in areas with unexpectedly low participation rates. For 2010, the Bureau set aside more than $7 million to rapidly target paid media in response to specific events leading up to the census or to areas with unexpectedly low mail participation rates.

Overall, the Bureau budgeted about $297.3 million on paid media in 2010, about $57 million (24 percent) more than in 2000 in constant 2010 dollars. The Bureau's 2010 paid media budget reflected several increases. On a unit cost basis, spending increased from an average of about $2.05 per housing unit in 2000 to $2.25 per housing unit in 2010, in constant 2010 dollars. Also, the Bureau increased the percentage of the budget for media development costs from 33 percent in 2000 to 43 percent in 2010. Table 1 compares the paid media spending in 2000 to 2010.

Table 1. Comparison of 2000 and 2010 Census Paid Media Budget

Component	2000 paid media[a] (in 2010 dollars)	2010 paid media[b]	Difference
Total paid media	$240,593,921	$297,346,773	$56,752,852 (24 percent)
Paid media development (production, labor, research, and other costs)	80,187,677	129,025,327	$48,837,650 (61 percent)
Paid media buys	160,406,244	168,321,446	$7,915,202 (4.9 percent)

Source: U.S. Census Bureau data.
[a] These are 2000 paid media actual costs.
[b] These are 2010 paid media estimated budget costs.

According to the Bureau, the cost increased for paid media development in part because of the extensive research done to target the media to specific groups and areas and because advertising was created in 12 more languages than in 2000. For example, to determine where paid media efforts may have the greatest impact, the Bureau developed predictive models based on 2000 census data and the evaluations of the partnership and paid media efforts from 2000. The models were provided to its contractor, DraftFCB, to aid in making paid media decisions. By better targeting paid media buys by area and message, the Bureau expected to more effectively reach those who have historically been the hardest to count. However, according to the Bureau, two factors—the use of evaluations from 2000 that did not isolate the impact of paid media from other components of the Bureau's outreach efforts, such as the partnership program, and the age of the data used—may have limited the model's ability to predict where paid media efforts had the greatest impact.

In a further effort to reach HTC groups, in 2010 the Bureau budgeted more for paid media that targeted HTC groups, like non-English-speaking audiences, than on the national audience, which was not the case in 2000, as shown in table 2.

Table 2. 2010 Census Paid Media Budget by Target Audience

Component	2000 paid media[a] (in 2010 dollars)	2010 paid media[b]	Difference
Total paid media buys	$160,406,244	$168,321,446	$7,915,202 (4.9 percent)
Mass audience (general population)	84,441,528	81,915,970	$-2,525,558 (-3 percent)
Ethnic/language audience	75,964,716	86,405,476	$10,440,760 (14 percent)

Source: U.S. Census Bureau data.
[a] These are 2000 paid media actual costs.
[b] These are 2010 paid media estimated budget costs.

Additionally, the Bureau strengthened its outreach efforts in 2010 by improving its monitoring and evaluation activities. For example, throughout the census the Bureau monitored the public's awareness and attitudes toward the census via surveys and by tracking relevant blogs. The Bureau used five sources of information, including national polls and actual mail participation rates, to monitor metrics such as individuals' understanding of the census, perceived benefits from participating in the census, and barriers to participating in the census. As a result, the Bureau used this information to identify markets and groups where additional outreach was needed. Table 3 compares key aspects of the 2000 and 2010 paid media activities.

Paid Media Used Market Research to Better Target HTC Populations

The Bureau generally implemented its 2010 paid media campaign as planned, targeting different segments of the HTC population. For example, to reach younger audiences, which are typically hard to count, the Bureau used new methods such as podcasts, YouTube videos, and social media networks

Table 3. Comparison of 2000 and 2010 Paid Media Activities

Paid media activities	2000 Census	2010 Census
Campaign development and targeting	Targeted advertisements by segmenting the population into three groups of census participation likelihood, based on measures of civic participation in an area, such as school board involvement.	Targeted advertisements based in part on actual 2000 participation rates and attitudinal research.
	Developed paid media messages in 16 languages.	Developed paid media messages in 28 languages.
	No electronic and Web-based communications made available.	Electronic and Web-based communications made available.
	Targeted the majority of paid media resources to national mass audience.	Targeted the majority of paid media resources to ethnic/non-English language audiences.
Implementation	Did not establish a media contingency fund for unexpected events.	Established a $7.4 million rapid response/media contingency fund to address unexpected events, such as lower response rates in certain areas.
Monitoring	Did not have the ability to measure the effectiveness of paid media during the census.	Used national polling and other methods to measure the effectiveness of paid media during the census.
Evaluation	Evaluated the impact of the communications campaign as a whole on awareness of the census.	Conducted controlled experiments measuring the impact of increased paid media exposure on mail response and made plans to evaluate the impact of individual components of the communications campaign, including paid media, on awareness and likelihood to participate in the census.

Source: GAO analysis of U.S. Census Bureau information.

such as Facebook and Twitter in addition to traditional TV and radio broadcasts. To reach people with limited English proficiency, the Bureau ran banner advertisements on, for example, Chinese language Web sites that linked directly to the Chinese language page of the Bureau's own Web site and targeted local radio advertisements to various ethnic audiences. Moreover, to reach audiences through their media habits and interests, the Bureau integrated census messages into regularly scheduled television programming in an attempt to appeal to people in new and more personal ways. For example, a Spanish-language soap opera made one of its characters an enumerator.

The Bureau also took advantage of its improved monitoring capacity and implemented a rapid response initiative to address markets with lagging mail participation rates or unforeseen events that might have affected response rates in certain markets. For example, as Census Day approached, the Bureau continuously tracked the public's attitudes toward the census to help determine the impact of its outreach activities. The Bureau found that while the percentage of people saying they would definitely participate in the census increased from about 50 percent in December 2009 to about 89 percent in March 2010, the data indicated that specific populations would have lower participation rates. As a result, the Bureau ran additional advertising targeted at the following groups, among others:

- 18- to 24-year-olds whose attitudes on their intent to participate in the census were not changing over time;
- English-speaking Hispanics who appeared less likely than Spanish-speaking Hispanics to understand the benefits of census participation; and
- Hasidic Jews in Brooklyn, New York, because mail participation rates were lagging in neighborhoods known to have significant Hasidic populations.

Further, in late March, the Bureau identified 23 specific media markets with mail participation rates significantly below the national average. Following rapid response efforts in these areas, 13 of these markets showed a significant increase in mail participation rates compared to the national average.

The Bureau originally budgeted $7.4 million for its rapid response efforts, but added approximately $28 million from a separate management reserve fund as data analysis showed a need for media intervention, for a total of about $35 million. Of this $35 million, about $31.8 million was allocated to new media purchases and about $3 million went to media production and other costs. Of the $31.8 million, the Bureau budgeted about $17.3 million (54 percent) of the rapid response paid media funding for the general population and $14.5 million (45 percent) for specific ethnic and language audiences.

The Bureau plans to assess the impact of the communications campaign on respondent attitudes and behaviors. For example, to determine how much it should invest in the paid media campaign, the Bureau held an experiment in 2010 where it flooded certain markets with more paid advertising than was used in other, similar markets. When the evaluation of this research is completed as scheduled in 2012, it could help the Bureau better determine whether greater levels of advertising would be cost-effective in terms of increasing the mail response rate of various races and ethnic groups. Moving forward, it will be important for the Bureau to use these evaluation results not only for planning 2020 Census-taking activities, but, as was the case for 2010, also for aiding in the development of a predictive model that could help the Bureau determine which media outlets provide the best return on investment in terms of raising awareness of the census and encouraging participation for specific demographic groups. The model could combine data from the 2000 and 2010 enumerations and inform allocation decisions for paid media.

Partnership Efforts Were More Comprehensive than in the 2000 Census

In designing the 2010 partnership program, the Bureau took a number of steps aimed at expanding its reach and addressing challenges from the 2000 Census. For example, in 2000, the Bureau hired about 600 partnership staff in the field who were responsible for mobilizing local support for the census by working with local organizations to promote census participation. However, we reported in 2001 that partnership specialists' heavy workload may have limited the level of support they were able to provide individual local census offices.[9] To help improve its ability to mobilize local support for 2010, the Bureau created a new position, the partnership assistant,[10] and hired about 2,800 partnership staff, about five times the number of partnership staff hired in 2000.[11] Thus, the Bureau increased the ratio of partnership staff per county and staff were not spread as thin.

Additionally, for 2000, the Bureau developed a database to track, plan, and analyze partnership efforts. We reported that the database was not user-friendly, which led to inefficiencies and duplication of effort.[12] For 2010, the Bureau revamped the partnership database to make it more user-friendly and to improve management's ability to use the information to monitor the progress of partnership activities. For example, while the 2000 database was mainly a catalog of census partner organizations, the 2010 database was designed to enable the Bureau to more actively manage the program in part by generating reports on value-added goods and services that partners provided, such as free training space. Table 4 compares key aspects of the 2000 and 2010 partnership activities.

Table 4. 2010 Partnership Activities Compared to Those in 2000

Partnership program activities	2000 Census	2010 Census
Implementation	Hired about 600 partnership staff.	Hired about 2,800 partnership staff.
	Recruited about 140,000 partner organizations.	Recruited more than 255,000 partner organizations.
	Partnership staff spoke 35 languages.	Partnership staff spoke 145 languages.
Monitoring	Did not establish real-time metrics to measure value-added and limited real-time tracking of partnership activities.	Established metrics to measure value-added contributions of partners and real-time tracking of partnership activities.
	Developed a partnership database to track partnership efforts. Bureau staff reported that the database was cumbersome and not user-friendly.	Revamped partnership database by, among other things, allowing for up-to-date monitoring of partner activity and a new Web-based interface.
Evaluation	Evaluated the impact of the communications campaign as a whole on awareness of the census, but had no ability to isolate the effect of partnership efforts.	Plans to evaluate the impact of individual components of the communications campaign on awareness of and likelihood to participate in the census, including the impact of the partnership program on raising awareness and affecting the participation rate.

Source: GAO analysis of U.S. Census Bureau information.

The Partnership Program Was Significantly Expanded, but Coordination and Monitoring Issues from 2000 Persisted

Aided by the Recovery Act funding that allowed the Bureau to increase its presence in local communities, the Bureau's outreach efforts resulted in recruiting over 100,000 more partners and increasing by over 100 the number of languages spoken by partnership staff. The Bureau estimated that it would spend about $280 million on partnership program costs from fiscal years 2007 through 2011, including $120 million from the Recovery Act—an increase of 54 percent from 2000.[13] To expand partnership activities in HTC areas, the Bureau used its allocation of Recovery Act-funded partnership staff in regions with large HTC populations. As a result, while in 2000 the average ratio was one partnership staff member for every five counties, in 2010 the average ratio was almost one partnership staff member for every county.

Partnership specialists conducted outreach activities that addressed the concerns of HTC communities in their areas. For example, one partnership specialist in the Atlanta region organized a conference of leaders in the Vietnamese community to ease their concerns about the confidentiality of census data. Another partnership specialist in the Los Angeles region leveraged the credibility of several large national Iranian and Arab organizations to help convince local community leaders that the census was mandated by law and that their constituents should complete and return census forms. Further, an LCOM in the Dallas region told us that partnership specialists worked to get a letter from the Mayor that helped enumerators gain access to local gated communities and apartment complexes.

Coordination Issues Persisted Despite Additional Bureau Guidance

During the 2000 Census, LCOMs we surveyed said that the reporting structure for partnership specialists may have led to communication and coordination hurdles between the partnership staff and local census office staff. As a result, we recommended that the Bureau explore ways to increase the coordination and communication between the partnership specialists and the LCOMs.[14] To address coordination and communication challenges in 2010, the Bureau developed additional guidance for partnership specialists and LCOMs, revised partnership training materials, and held meetings between regional operations staff and partnership staff to discuss ways to enhance communications. For example, the Bureau revised the LCOMs' handbook to explain that partnership specialists and local census office staff have a responsibility to work together to ensure that they do not duplicate each others' efforts. In addition, the partnership training manual specifically stated that partnership specialists should participate in local census office management meetings, provide management teams with their schedules of planned meetings and activities in advance, and update LCOMs on their completed activities.

Moreover, most of the partnership staff we interviewed reported working closely or having mutually supportive relationships with local census office staff. For example, partnership staff in the Atlanta and Charlotte regions said that they attended training with local census office staff, and one partnership specialist told us that training gave them a better understanding of the roles and responsibilities of local census offices.

However, LCOMs we surveyed provided a more mixed view of the coordination and communication between the partnership program and local census offices. On the one hand, 39 percent of 395 LCOMs responding to our March survey said they were generally or very satisfied with partnership staff's assistance with local challenges.[15] In addition, some managers provided positive comments in the open ended section of the survey about partnership staff's assistance. For example, one LCOM commented that partnership staff assisted with local census office recruiting activities, such as setting up and providing materials for promotional events. In another example, a manager from the Boston region said that the local census office staff and the partnership specialist worked as one team and contributed to the success of the census. These results varied regionally, with more satisfaction in the Bureau's Boston, Los Angeles, and Dallas regions than in the Philadelphia and New York regions.

On the other hand, the results of our survey of LCOMs also highlight areas for improvement. In March, 50 percent of 393 LCOMs responding said they were generally or very dissatisfied with coordination between local census offices and partnership staff and a similar level of dissatisfaction was found in a follow-up survey we conducted in May after the nonresponse follow-up operation started.[16] Among the responses of those LCOMs who elaborated on their satisfaction with coordination between local census offices and partnership staff, a key theme was a lack of cooperation or interaction between the partnership and local census office staffs. A manager from the Chicago region said that though the partnership specialist was good, the organizational structure and upper management did not allow for proper interaction. The manager said that at first, communication between the local census office staff and the partnership specialist was prohibited by the partnership specialist team leader, which impeded the local census office's ability to make valuable community connections.

One reason for the coordination challenges between local census offices and partnership staff could be their different reporting structures. As shown in figure 1, LCOMs and partnership specialists report to different officials, and the official who oversees both positions is two levels above the LCOM and three levels above the partnership specialist.

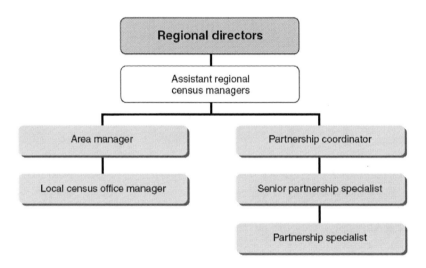

Figure 1. Reporting Structure for Regional Census Centers.

According to Bureau officials, this reporting structure was established to allow partnership specialists to coordinate their efforts with other partnership specialists in the same geographical areas and share common problems and solutions. Further, some partnership specialists were responsible for reaching out to specific ethnic groups in areas covered by different local census offices, making it logistically difficult for the specialists to report to one local census office.

But among the LCOMs who elaborated on their responses to our survey, a key theme was dissatisfaction with this reporting structure. For example, one manager reported that the partnership program and local census office operations are too disconnected, adding that at times both partnership staff and local census office staff were doing the same tasks. The manager said that the partnership program was an essential part of a successful census, but only when performed in conjunction with local census office operations. Another manager said that the partnership program needs a direct link to the local census office and suggested that a position such as an assistant manager for partnership be added to the local census office staff. Such a position, the manager explained, would solidify the communication between the partnership program and the local census office.

Regardless of the management structure, what is clear is that more positive experiences seemed to result when LCOMs and partnership specialists dovetailed their efforts. Better communication between partnership specialists and LCOMs may have enhanced the Bureau's capacity to reduce duplicative efforts, close any gaps in outreach to community organizations with significant HTC populations, and leverage opportunities to achieve a more complete and accurate count.

Despite Revamping, the Partnership Database Remained Problematic

The partnership tracking database could also benefit from refinements. Despite improvements, partnership staff raised concerns about its user-friendliness similar to those reported in 2000. In 2010, all the partnership specialists we interviewed reported that data entry was time consuming, and 8 of the 11 partnership staff we interviewed reported that they needed help with data entry in order to keep the database current. The Bureau expected to use the partnership database to more accurately monitor and improve partnership efforts nationally; thus the difficulty partnership staff found in updating the system is noteworthy.

Initially, no partnership assistants were authorized to access the database because the Bureau wanted to ensure that data were entered into the system consistently. The Bureau was also concerned about the additional costs associated with purchasing licenses for the large number of partnership assistants. However, in response to regional partnership staff's concerns over the partnership specialists' struggles to update the database in a timely manner, the Bureau procured approximately 400 licenses for select partnership assistants in August 2009. But in interviews with partnership specialists from March through May 2010, they told us that they continued to experience difficulty meeting the data entry requirements.

Further, Bureau managers could not be sure if information in the partnership database was up-to-date. Bureau officials told us that they expected partnership specialists to immediately log any contact they had with a partner into the database. However, our analysis of reports from the database showed, on average, that about 35 percent of users did not update the database on a weekly basis from March 4 through April 22, 2010. According to Bureau headquarters officials responsible for managing the partnership program, because the partnership data were not always current, they took the extra step of organizing weekly telephone calls between headquarters and regional partnership staff in order to gain the most up-to-date information on partnership activities. More current information during a crucial time period around Census Day, April 1, could have better positioned the Bureau to quickly identify and address problem areas. Further, Bureau managers would likely have had better data for redeploying partnership resources to low responding areas with significant HTC populations during different census operations.

Aligning the Delivery of Promotional Materials with the Hiring of Partnership Staff Could Foster More Effective Relationships with Partner Organizations

Although the Bureau developed English and foreign language promotional materials—both in hard copy and for the Bureau's Web page—for partnership specialists and assistants to use when recruiting partner organizations, the materials were not available when partnership specialists were first hired. Eight of the 11 partnership specialists and assistants we interviewed reported that because promotional materials were not available when needed, it was more difficult for them to build relationships with potential partners. Specifically, the Bureau began hiring partnership specialists in January 2008. However, delivery of the promotional materials did not start until April 2009, more than a year after partnership specialists first came on board. Although this still left a year until Census Day, by not having promotional materials on hand when partnership staff first began their work, the Bureau may have missed opportunities to develop and strengthen relationships with organizations that had the ability to influence census participation among HTC groups.

Further, three of the eight partnership staff who worked with non-English-speaking communities said it was difficult to obtain in-language materials when needed. For example, one partnership employee in the Los Angeles region reported being unable to engage Korean churches until after January 2010 when the needed in-language materials first became available (according to Bureau officials, in-language materials took longer to develop than English language materials because of the need to ensure accurate translations).

Bureau officials acknowledged that the schedule for hiring partnership staff and the delivery of promotional materials were not well aligned. In the interim, the Bureau provided partnership staff with talking points to help them reach out to organizations in the early phase of the program.

Moving forward, it will be important for the Bureau to take a fresh look at recurring problems in the partnership program, as well as reconsider time frames for the availability of promotional materials. Through improving communication and coordination between partnership and local census office staff, developing a user-friendly database to more effectively monitor the program's progress, and ensuring that promotional materials are available for distribution when partnership specialists are first hired, the Bureau would better position itself to promote the census to HTC populations.

THE BUREAU ENHANCED ENUMERATION PROGRAMS AIMED AT HTC GROUPS; ADDITIONAL REFINEMENTS COULD IMPROVE THEM FOR 2020

Aspects of 2010 SBE Were Refined to Address Implementation Issues from 2000 and Better Enumerate HTC Groups

To improve its ability to count individuals without conventional housing, the Bureau made a number of improvements to SBE, many of which were designed to address challenges experienced in 2000. For example, in 2000, SBE enumerators were not trained to enumerate all types of SBE facilities, which limited the times when enumeration could occur. In response to service providers' requests for more flexibility on scheduling enumeration during the 3-day operation, the Bureau trained census workers to enumerate all types of SBE facilities. This change made training more consistent nationwide and enabled the Bureau to better accommodate last-minute schedule changes.

Further, in some cases in 2000, the supply of census forms and training materials provided to the local offices was not adequate. In 2010, the Bureau reduced the number of form types used for enumerating individuals at SBE facilities from four to a single multipurpose form. According to Bureau officials, this change allowed them to provide an adequate number of forms to local census offices and also helped increase efficiency.

The Bureau took several steps that helped it identify a larger number of SBE facilities in 2010 than in 2000, thereby positioning the Bureau to conduct a more complete count. The actual number of SBE facilities the Bureau enumerated in 2000 was 14,817, whereas for 2010 the Bureau had plans to enumerate 64,626 sites—four times more than previously enumerated.[17] The

Table 5. Comparison of 2000 and 2010 SBE Operations

SBE activities	2000 Census	2010 Census
Planning and training	Used four different types of questionnaires to enumerate SBE facilities.	Used one questionnaire to minimize confusion and facilitatethe availability of supplies in a timely manner.
	Did not consolidate training for SBE facilities.	Consolidated training for staff enumerating people living in group situations such as those in SBE facilities, thereby enabling enumerators to work on multiple operations and all types of SBE facilities.
	Questionnaires and training materials were insufficient, untimely, or both.	Materials were generally timely and sufficient.
	Conducted advance visits to identify the population to be enumerated and issues that could affect enumeration.	Same as 2000.
	Made no additions to list of SBE facilities and TNSOLs after the enumeration date.	Allowed additions to list of SBE facilities and TNSOLs through the last day of SBE enumeration.
	Allowed no flexibility for facilities on when they would be enumerated.	Provided facilities with flexibility on when they would be enumerated.
	Identified SBE sites by working with local governments and community-based organizations, reviewing facility listings from other census operations, and having local staff review the yellow pages.	Expanded efforts to identify SBE sites by providing partnership staff with more guidance, including identifying TNSOLs, and by having headquarters staff work more closely with regional and local staff to develop a more complete list.
Evaluation	Assessment included an examination of duplicate questionnaires and quality assurance procedures. Used results for future planning.	Assessment will include (1) final workload volumes, costs, and quality assurance results; (2) information collected from debriefings; and (3) lessons learned. Plans to use results for future planning.

Source: GAO analysis of U.S. Census Bureau information.

steps included working more closely with local and national partner organizations and assigning partnership assistants a role in identifying service-providing facilities. The Bureau also developed better guidance for partnership assistants to identify TNSOLs, relying in part on input from partner organizations, such as church groups and service providers that were familiar with outdoor areas where people often spent the night. Further, the Bureau used public mailings and technology, such as the Internet, to find a broader spectrum of facilities, as compared to local telephone listings that were used in 2000. Table 5 compares key aspects of the 2000 and 2010 SBE operations.

The Bureau Generally Implemented SBE Consistent with Its Operation Plans but Experienced Continuing Challenges

The Bureau generally implemented the SBE operation as planned, completing the 3-day operation on schedule, and spending $10.9 million, slightly more than the $10.6 million budgeted for the operation. However, while the overall budget estimate for the 2010 SBE operation was more accurate than in 2000, the actual costs for local census offices in urban HTC areas was almost double the amount budgeted—$1.9 million compared to the actual cost of $3.6 million.[18] Bureau officials said they will examine the data further to determine why the budget was exceeded in urban HTC areas. We have noted the Bureau's difficulties in developing accurate cost estimates for several other Bureau operations, and the cost overrun in urban HTC areas is another example of this.[19]

As in 2000, our observers noted that enumerators were professional, responsible, knowledgeable, and highly committed to fulfilling their responsibilities. For example, during heavy rain in the Boston area, enumerators remained focused on counting individuals living under overhangs and stairwells, despite the difficult conditions. Our observers in Brooklyn reported the same of enumerators there, although enumeration of the outdoor locations was delayed one night because of adverse weather conditions. Further, one of our observers reported that in Los Angeles, cultural advocates—individuals the Bureau hired to accompany enumerators and facilitate access to certain communities—helped ease potentially tense situations.

As described below, based on our observations and the results of the LCOM survey, SBE generally went well, and in some areas the Bureau appears to have addressed challenges it experienced in 2000.

Enumeration Supplies Were Generally Adequate

Enumerators we spoke with reported having enough forms in 68 of 78 sites we visited. Also, 76 percent of 359 LCOMs who responded to our question on the timing of the delivery of questionnaires and other enumerations supplies were generally or very satisfied. In contrast, during the 2000 Census, our observers noted that the timing of questionnaires and training materials was not always adequate at the locations they visited, which impeded enumerators' ability to conduct their work in a timely manner.

Advanced Visits Helped Enhance Service Providers' Readiness for Enumeration

Our observers reported that facilities were prepared for SBE enumeration in 35 of 56 visits to SBE facilities. Furthermore, 73 percent of 356 LCOMs who responded to our question about the readiness of SBE facilities were generally or very satisfied. In instances where facilities were not prepared, there appears to have been an expectation or communication gap. Despite advance visits from the Bureau, one representative at a Baltimore facility Our observers reported that facilities were prepared for SBE enumeration in 35 of 56 visits to SBE facilities. Furthermore, 73 percent of 356 LCOMs who responded to our question about the readiness of SBE facilities were generally or very satisfied. In instances where facilities were not prepared, there appears to have been an expectation or communication gap. Despite advance visits from the Bureau, one representative at a Baltimore facility said she was not aware that census workers were expected, and would not allow enumeration to take place because it would disrupt the individuals' dinner and medication treatments. She was not receptive to the workers returning later the same evening. In another case, a Boston facility manager was not aware that the enumeration was to take place, but allowed the census workers to proceed. Bureau officials said that in some instances facility staff may not have communicated previous agreements for conducting the enumeration to new or other staff on duty at the time of the enumeration.

Training Material Was Tailored to Accommodate Local Conditions

Of the LCOMs we surveyed, 65 percent of 359 LCOMs were generally or very satisfied that the content of SBE training materials was tailored to accommodate local conditions, such as taking into account whether an area was urban or rural. In 2000, enumerators expressed concern that the training they received did not always adequately prepare them for the wide range of scenarios they encountered.

Despite these successes, the Bureau experienced some procedural and operational challenges during SBE implementation, some of which were similar to the Bureau's experience in 2000.

Enumerators Did Not Always Follow Procedures

The Bureau's policy referred to in its SBE enumeration manual stipulates that when individuals state that they have already been enumerated elsewhere, the enumerator still must attempt to complete a questionnaire.[20] While enumerators adhered to this procedure at about two-thirds of the facilities we visited, we found that in 26 of 78 visits enumerators did not attempt to enumerate individuals who told them they had already completed a questionnaire at another location. When individuals refuse to be enumerated, regardless of the reason, the Bureau'sguidance instructs enumerators to ask the facility's contact person for information about the individual. If a contact person is not available, the enumerator should attempt to complete as much of the questionnaire as possible through observation. By not always following these procedures, enumerators may have missed individuals who should have been enumerated and the extent to which accuracy of the count was affected is unknown.

Enumerators Did Not Always Fulfill Agreements

As mentioned previously, Bureau officials visited SBE facilities to make agreements with service providers on conducting the actual enumeration. Our observers noted that in 15 of 78 site visits, enumerators did not arrive as scheduled at shelter locations. One of these instances occurred in Washington, D.C., where the facility manager had instructed the clientele who typically frequent that location to make an effort to be present when the enumerator arrived. According to the facility manager, the enumerator did not arrive at the scheduled time. In another instance, a facility manager at a Boston site told our observers that she was concerned that enumerators had arrived earlier than the agreed-upon time. She explained that her clientele consisted of emotionally disturbed women, many of whom had fears of authority. Thus, she said she would have preferred more time to prepare the women for the impending visit.

When enumerators do not fulfill commitments, the missed appointments and the need to reschedule could make the enumeration more burdensome to service providers and detract from the Bureau's reputation.

Determining Appropriate Staffing Levels for SBE Sites Was Sometimes Problematic

The mobile nature of the SBE population and other factors make it difficult to precisely determine the number of enumerators that should be sent to a particular site, and sending either too many or too few enumerators each has its consequences. Although the Bureau has guidance on staffing ratios for enumerating different types of group quarters, including service-based facilities, it did not always result in optimal levels of staffing at shelters and TNSOLs. Overstaffing can lead to unnecessarily higher labor costs and poor productivity, while understaffing can affect the Bureau's ability to obtain a complete count at a particular site.

Our observers and those in the Department of Commerce's Office of Inspector General both reported overstaffing as an issue at SBE locations. For example, at one of our SBE site visits, approximately 30 enumerators reported to the same shelter in Atlanta to conduct the enumeration. Unsure of how to proceed, the census enumerators waited for over an hour before a crew leader instructed over half of the enumerators present to leave, at which point no work had taken place. Similarly, the Department of Commerce Inspector General's staff observed long periods of inactivity at sites and increased operational costs as a result.[21]

Also, while most LCOMs we surveyed were satisfied with SBE staffing levels, pockets of dissatisfaction existed at some locations. Of the LCOMs responding to our survey in April, 81 percent of 361 were generally or very satisfied with the number of enumerators hired to complete the SBE workload, 10 percent of managers said they were generally or very dissatisfied, and 9 percent of managers said they were neither satisfied nor dissatisfied. Of the responses from managers who elaborated on our question about their satisfaction level with the SBE operation, a key theme that emerged was overstaffing. One manager, elaborating on his response, said that he sent a detailed cost and benefit document to higher-level Bureau officials to demonstrate that the number of enumerators needed for the SBE operation in his local area should be reduced, but his request was denied. In another instance, a manager said he was required to train and hire at least 100 more enumerators than he felt were necessary.

Given the Bureau's constitutional mandate to enumerate the country's entire population and the difficulty of enumerating the SBE population, it is not unreasonable for the Bureau to err on the side of over- rather than understaffing SBE to help ensure a complete count. Going forward, as part of the Bureau's plans to examine SBE costs, schedule, training, and staffing, it will be important for the Bureau to determine the factors that led to less-than-optimal staffing levels and use the information to help determine staffing levels for SBE in 2020.

Be Counted/QAC Programs Were Implemented as Planned, but Visibility Issues Remain a Concern

For 2010, the Bureau developed plans that according to Bureau officials, were designed to address challenges that the Be Counted/QAC programs faced during the 2000 Census, such as (1) visibility of sites, (2) ability of the public to find where the Be Counted/QAC sites were located, and (3) monitoring of site activity. In 2000, for example, several sites we visited lacked signs publicizing the sites' existence, which greatly reduced visibility. In some sites, census questionnaires were in places where people might not look for them, such as the bottom of a shelf. We reported that the Bureau had problems with keeping site information current, and as a result, changes in the information about the program's site location or points of contact were not always available to the public.[22] To address these issues, in 2010, the Bureau created banners for display in public areas of Be Counted/QAC sites, developed a Web page with locations and hours of the sites, and updated the guidance for site selection. Table 6 compares key aspects of the 2000 and 2010 Be Counted/QAC programs.

The Bureau generally implemented the Be Counted/QAC program as planned. The Bureau opened around 38,000 sites, conducted the Be Counted/QAC program as scheduled from March 19 through April 19,[23] and completed the Be Counted/QAC program under budget. The Bureau reported spending $38.7 million versus the $44.2 million budgeted. Bureau officials commented that the program came in under budget in part because the Bureau staffed the sites with one QAC representative for 15 hours a week, rather than with 1.5 representatives, as originally budgeted. This allowed the Bureau to spend less on payroll and training, according to officials.

Overall, the majority of the 51 sites we visited were staffed as planned and census materials and forms were available at most sites in multiple languages. Further, the Bureau's preliminary data on 2010 show overall activity at Be Counted/QAC sites increased, with about 1 million more forms picked up in 2010, compared to the approximately 1.7 million forms in 2000—an increase of 62 percent.

Table 6. Comparison of 2000 and 2010 Be Counted/QAC Programs

Be Counted/ QAC activities	2000 Census	2010 Census
Planning and site selection	Selected sites via a joint effort between partnership specialists and partner organizations. No role for local census office staff.	Selected sites via joint effort between partnership specialists and local census office staff with input from partner organizations.
Implementation	Had a goal to establish about 66,000 locations. Census data indicated that 28,632 were established.	Had a goal to establish 40,000 Be Counted and QAC sites. Census preliminary data indicated that 38,827 sites were established.
	Staffed sites with paid employees and volunteers, which led to inconsistent service.	Staffed sites solely with paid employees to ensure consistent service.
	Forms available in 6 languages—English, Spanish, Chinese, Korean, Vietnamese, and Tagalog. Language assistance guides available in 37 languages.	Forms available in 6 languages—English, Spanish, Chinese, Vietnamese, Korean, and Russian. Language assistance guides available in 59 languages.
	Did not provide Web page for public to locate Be Counted/QAC locations.	Established a Web page that helped the public locate Be Counted/QAC locations.
	Did not issue official signage identifying Be Counted/QAC sites.	Issued uniform signage for prominent display at sites.
Monitoring	Attempted to monitor site performance, but the number of Be Counted/QAC sites was more than could be handled.	Monitored sites by designating Be Counted clerks in local census offices to regularly visit sites and check staffing and adequacy of materials.
Evaluation	Relied on cost and workload data.	Same as 2000.
	Assessment included final workload volumes, costs, and quality assurance results. Used for future planning.	Same as 2000.

Source: GAO analysis of U.S. Census Bureau information.

Visibility of Be Counted/QAC Sites Was Poor at Many Sites Visited

Visibility is key to the effectiveness of Be Counted/QAC sites because it is directly related to people's ability to find them. According to the Bureau's Be Counted job aid guidance, Be Counted clerks in local census offices were responsible for monitoring sites and ensuring that banners were displayed at Be Counted/QAC locations. In many locations we visited, the Bureau's efforts to raise the visibility of sites were evident to our observers. For example, 23 of the 51 Be Counted/QAC sites visited were displaying the banners the Bureau developed to advertise the existence of the Be Counted/QAC sites. More generally, however, there were areas for improvement. For example, our observers noted problems with "street-level" visibility in 26 of 51 Be Counted/QAC sites visited. At one site in Atlanta, for instance, no signs were visible from the main road to publicize the existence of the Be Counted site. In addition, our observers visited two sites in Brooklyn that were not visible from the street. In some cases, the banners provided by the Bureau to advertise the location of a site were not used or displayed prominently upon entering a location that housed a site. At another site in Washington, D.C., our observers noted that the banner was rolled up and leaning against a file cabinet and consequently was not clearly visible to the public.

Source: GAO.

Figure 2. Be Counted Forms Prominently Displayed at Brooklyn Be Counted/QAC Site.

2010 Census: Key Efforts to Include Hard-to-Count Populations ... 101

In addition, Be Counted/QAC sites were sometimes in obscure locations within the buildings in which they were housed. For example, at sites located in the basement or rear of the building, we observed no signage directing people to the Be Counted/QAC site. Further, forms and materials available at Be Counted/QAC sites were not always clearly identified and thus could have been overlooked. Figure 2 is an example of a Be Counted site in Brooklyn that was prominently visible at a library. Importantly, the banner was clearly displayed to draw attention to the site, and the time that staff would be in attendance was also obvious.

In contrast, figure 3 shows a Be Counted site in Fresno, California, that was difficult to find in a barbershop. Note that the area had no signage to draw attention to the site and the forms were scattered about and difficult to find.

Figure 3. Be Counted Forms Not Prominently Displayed at Fresno Be Counted/QAC Site.

In those instances when the Be Counted/QAC sites were not clearly visible to the public, the Bureau may have missed one of the last opportunities to directly enumerate individuals. Moving forward, the Bureau should consider more effective ways to monitor site visibility at Be Counted/QAC sites. For example, the Bureau could include visibility as one of the areas to monitor when census staff conduct their regular monitoring of the Be Counted sites.

Site Selection Guidance Does Not Consider Potential Activity Levels

Along with visibility, the procedures used to select Be Counted/QAC sites are also key to the effectiveness of the program because they affect the extent to which sites are easily accessible to targeted populations. To improve selection of Be Counted/QAC sites in 2010, the Bureau revised its guidance on Be Counted/QAC site criteria by emphasizing locating sites in HTC areas and specifying the types of local census office areas where sites should be located (e.g., urban/HTC and urban/metropolitan). However, the guidance did not provide direction on identifying sites in locations with the likelihood of higher levels of activity, which would increase the potential for individuals to pick up Be Counted forms. Moreover, Bureau officials said they encouraged staff to take advantage of locations that were free of charge as well as locations with the likelihood of higher levels of activity.

Activity levels at the Be Counted/QAC sites varied based on information from Bureau staff and our observations. QAC representatives at 8 of 43 QAC-only sites visited told us that their sites had moderate to high levels of activity while 12 of 43 QAC representatives told us their sites had low levels of activity.[24] For example, a QAC representative at one facility in Phoenix and another in Atlanta said they had to frequently restock Be Counted forms and that they provided many people with assistance. Another QAC representative in Dallas said that he assisted up to 30 people in one day at the Be Counted/QAC site he staffed. Conversely, a QAC representative in Miami said that the LCOM was considering the site for closure because very few people visited the location and used the services. Similarly, a firefighter at a Dallas QAC site observed that the site was open for 11 days and no one visited the site during this time and the box containing materials accompanying the questionnaires (i.e., pens and language reference documents) was unopened. Additionally, during a June debriefing, where QAC representatives discussed their experiences with Bureau officials, the QAC representatives commented on the problem of low activity at some Be Counted/QAC sites, according to Bureau officials.

Preliminary data on forms returned and checked in also revealed changes in activity levels at Be Counted/QAC sites for 2010. For example, an average of 20 forms were returned and checked in from each Be Counted/QAC site in 2010, down from an average of 28 in 2000. Given that the operation was conducted over a 30-day period, that translates to less than 1 form per day per site. While this difference might reflect the fact that the address list in 2010 was better than in 2000 and that fewer households were missed, it also indicates that the operation was very resource intensive relative to the number of forms that were returned.

According to Bureau planning guidance, both local census office staff and partnership specialists were jointly responsible for identifying Be Counted/QAC sites, and local census office staff were responsible for monitoring the sites. However, a number of LCOMs we surveyed in May expressed concern about assistance from partnership specialists in identifying Be Counted/QAC sites. While 32 percent of 369 LCOMs who responded to our survey were generally or very satisfied with the assistance they received from partnership specialists for identifying sites, 57 percent of managers responding indicated that they were generally or very dissatisfied. Among the responses of those LCOMs who elaborated on their satisfaction level with the partnership program, one key theme that emerged was dissatisfaction with the Be Counted/QAC sites identified. For example, one LCOM commented that many of the Be Counted/QAC sites were in poor locations and were not in areas with the highest need. To the extent that the Be Counted/QAC sites were established in locations with low activity, the result was lower productivity and higher costs to the Bureau in the form of wages paid to census employees to staff and monitor the sites. There were also opportunity costs in monitoring a site with low activity when a site in a different location could have produced better results.

The Be Counted/QAC program, in concept, may be a reasonable effort to include people who might have otherwise been missed by the census. However, it was also a resource-intensive operation in which relatively few questionnaires, on average per site, were generated, once the cost and effort of identifying, stocking, staffing, monitoring, and maintaining the sites are considered. More will be known about the effectiveness of the Be Counted/QAC program when the Bureau determines how many Be Counted/QAC forms resulted in adding people and new addresses to the census. Similar to SBE, the Bureau plans to assess the Be Counted/QAC program by examining costs, schedule, training, and staffing. Moving forward, it will also be important for the Bureau to explore ways to maximize the Be

Counted/QAC program's ability to increase the number of forms returned and checked in from the target population for the 2020 Census and, ultimately, determine whether fewer but more strategically placed sites could produce more cost-effective results.

CONCLUSIONS

In 2010, the Bureau was better positioned to reach out to and enumerate HTC populations compared to 2000 in large part because its plans addressed a number of the challenges experienced in the previous decennial. For example, the Bureau focused more of its resources on targeting paid media efforts to HTC groups, employed partnership staff with a wider range of language capabilities, and developed a more comprehensive list of service-providing facilities that likely enhanced its capacity to enumerate people lacking conventional housing. Further, from an operational perspective, the Bureau generally implemented its HTC outreach and enumeration efforts consistent with its operational plans, completing them within schedule and budget. Overall, while the full impact of these efforts will not be known until after the Bureau completes various assessments, including an evaluation of the extent and nature of any under- and overcounts, the Bureau's rigorous effort to raise awareness, encourage participation, and enumerate HTC populations likely played a key role in holding mail participation rates steady in 2010 for the overall population, a significant achievement given the various factors that were acting against an acceptable mail response in 2010.

Still, certain aspects of the Bureau's outreach and enumeration of HTC populations need attention. Key focus areas for outreach efforts include (1) ensuring the Bureau is using paid media efficiently to improve response rates, (2) improving the coordination between partnership and local census office staff to leverage opportunities to achieve a more accurate and complete count, (3) improving the partnership database to enhance its use as a management tool, and (4) making promotional materials available to partnership staff when they begin their work to improve their ability to develop relationships with partner organizations. For enumeration activities, by determining the factors that lead to the SBE staffing issues at some locations and revising site selection guidance for Be Counted/QAC sites based on visitation and other applicable data, the Bureau may increase the overall value of special enumeration activities.

More generally, the Bureau invested more resources in reaching out to and enumerating HTC groups in 2010 but achieved the same overall participation rate as in 2000. This trend is likely to continue as the nation's population gets larger, more diverse, and more difficult to count. As the Bureau looks toward the next national headcount, it plans to use the results of its evaluations for input into 2020 planning. At the same time, it will be important for the Bureau to go beyond that and use 2010 evaluation results to gain a better understanding of the extent to which the various special enumeration activities aimed at HTC groups produced a more complete and accurate census. More specifically, better information on the value added by each special enumeration activity could help the Bureau allocate its resources more cost effectively. This may include changing existing programs to increase efficiency or undertaking new special enumeration efforts altogether.

RECOMMENDATIONS FOR EXECUTIVE ACTION

To help improve the effectiveness of the Bureau's outreach and enumeration efforts, especially for HTC populations, should they be used again in the 2020 Census, we recommend that the Secretary of Commerce require the Under Secretary for Economic Affairs as well as the Director of the U.S. Census Bureau to take the following seven actions:

To improve the Bureau's marketing/outreach efforts:

- Use evaluation results, response rate, and other data to develop a predictive model that would inform decisions on how much and how best to allocate paid media funds for 2020.
- Develop mechanisms to increase coordination and communication between the partnership and local census office staff. Possible actions include offering more opportunities for joint training, establishing protocols for coordination, and more effectively leveraging the partnership contact database to better align partnership outreach activities with local needs.
- Improve the user-friendliness of the partnership database to help ensure more timely updates of contact information and enhance its use as a management tool.
- Ensure that promotional materials, including in-language materials for the partnership program, are available when partnership staff are first hired.

To improve some of the Bureau's key efforts to enumerate HTC populations:

- Assess visitation, response rate, and other applicable data on Be Counted/QAC locations and use that information to revise site selection guidance for 2020.
- Determine the factors that led to the staffing issues observed during SBE and take corrective actions to ensure more efficient SBE staffing levels in 2020.
- Evaluate the extent to which each special enumeration activity improved the count of traditionally hard-to-enumerate groups and use the results to help inform decision making on spending for these programs in 2020.

AGENCY COMMENTS AND OUR EVALUATION

On December 8, 2010, the Secretary of Commerce provided written comments on the draft report, which are reprinted in appendix I. The Department of Commerce generally agreed with the overall findings and recommendations of the report. In addition, the department noted that its Economics and Statistics Administration (ESA) has management oversight responsibility for the Bureau and asked that we include ESA in our recommendation. We revised the report to reflect this comment.

Appendix I: Comments from the Department of Commerce

December 8, 2010

Mr. Robert Goldenkoff
Director
Strategic Issues
United States Government Accountability Office
Washington, DC 20548

Dear Mr. Goldenkoff:

The Department of Commerce appreciates the opportunity to comment on the United States Government Accountability Office (GAO) draft report titled "2010 Census: Key Efforts to Include Hard-to-Count Populations Went Generally as Planned; Improvements Could Make the Efforts More Effective for Next Census" (GAO 11-45). Our comments on this report are enclosed.

Sincerely,

Gary Locke

Enclosures

United States Government Accountability Office

Department of Commerce
Comments on the
United States Government Accountability Office
Draft Report Titled
"2010 Census: Key Efforts to Include Hard-to-Count Populations Went Generally as Planned;
Improvements Could Make the Efforts More Effective for Next Census"
(GAO 11-45)
December 2010

The Department of Commerce thanks the GAO for their extensive efforts in examining these 2010 Census activities and for their ongoing efforts to help us develop a successful plan for the 2020 Census.

The Census Bureau generally agrees with the overall findings in this report and with the recommendations regarding matters we should study for the 2020 Census. Our comments follow.

- Page 44, first paragraph: "...we recommend that the Secretary of Commerce require the Director of the U.S. Census Bureau to take the following seven actions:..."

    Response: The Secretary of Commerce should require the Under Secretary for Economic Affairs as well as the Census Director. The Under Secretary heads the Economics and Statistics Administration (ESA), which has management oversight responsibility for the Census Bureau and has been actively engaged in planning for the 2020 Census.

- Page 45, second paragraph from bottom of page: "We are sending copies of this report to the Secretary of Commerce, the Director of the U.S. Census Bureau, and interested congressional committees."

    Response: Please also send a copy of the report to the Under Secretary for Economic Affairs.

End Notes

[1] The differential undercount describes subpopulations that are undercounted at a different rate than the total population.

[2] The 2000 mail participation rate was 74 percent for the short-form only. In 2000, the census included a long-form that asked for information that was not included on the short-form. The 2000 mail participation rate when including both the long-form and the short-form was 69 percent. The 2010 census did not use a long-form.

[3] GAO, *2010 Census: Data Collection Operations Were Generally Completed as Planned, but Long-standing Challenges Suggest Need for Fundamental Reforms*, GAO-11-193 (Washington, D.C.: Dec. 14, 2010). GAO, *2010 Census: Follow-up Should Reduce Coverage Errors, but Effects on Demographic Groups Need to be Determined*, GAO-11-154 (Washington, D.C.: Dec. 14, 2010). For additional products, see the Related GAO Products section at the end of this report.

[4] The other approximately 5 percent of the communications campaign budget was targeted to public relations, at about 3.9 percent ($25,610,360), and the Census in Schools Program, at about 1.7 percent ($11,320,000).

[5] Additionally, we visited local census offices in Atlanta, Baltimore, Brooklyn, Fresno, Miami, Phoenix, San Francisco and Washington, D.C. The Bureau had 494 local census offices nationwide. Local census offices recruited and trained enumerators and checked in completed questionnaires, among other tasks.

[6] The Integrated Partnership Contact Database tracks and monitors activities of partner organizations. Available in January 2009, the database contains real-time information on the number of partner organizations, populations served, demographics, value-added contributions, and constituent reach.

[7] Pub. L. No. 111-5, div. A, tit. II, 123 Stat. 115, 127. The Bureau received $1 billion from the Recovery Act. In the conference report accompanying the Act, the conferees stated that "of the amounts provided, up to $250,000,000 shall be for partnership and outreach efforts to minority communities and hard-to-reach populations." H.R. Conf. Rep. No. 116-16 at 417 (2009). According to the Bureau, it planned to use $220 million for expanding the communications campaign, out of this amount, $120 million was to enhance the partnership program. The Bureau planned to use $30 million for expanding its coverage follow-up operation, where census workers follow up to resolve conflicting information provided on census forms.

[8] Cases where the respondents indicated that they had no usual address will be assigned to higher-level geographic units, such as state and county, and are allocated to census counts accordingly.

[9] GAO, *2000 Census: Review of Partnership Program Highlights Best Practices for Future Operations*, GAO-01-579 (Washington, D.C.: Aug. 20, 2001).

[10] Partnership assistants were responsible for assisting partnership specialists in scheduling and conducting outreach activities.

[11] The staffing level was substantially higher than the Bureau originally planned for 2010 because of additional funds used to enhance the partnership program from the Recovery Act. See footnote 7.

[12] GAO-01-579.

[13] From October 1997 through September 2000, the Bureau spent about $182 million on its partnership program in constant 2010 dollars.

[14] GAO-01-579.

[15] The number of managers who responded to individual survey questions varied by question.

[16] Nonresponse follow-up is the largest and most costly field operation, where census workers follow up in person with households that did not respond to the census forms that were mailed to them.

[17] At the time of our work, the Bureau had not yet produced a final number of facilities actually enumerated.

[18] In 2000, the budget for SBE, in constant 2010 dollars, was $52.2 million, and the expended amount, in constant 2010 dollars, was $12.1 million. Budgeted and actual dollars spent for 2000 and 2010 were rounded.

[19] GAO, *2010 Census: Efforts to Build an Accurate Address List Are Making Progress, but Face Software and Other Challenges*, GAO-10-140T (Washington, D.C.: Oct. 21, 2009), and *2010 Census: Census Bureau Should Take Action to Improve the Credibility and Accuracy of Its Cost Estimate for the Decennial Census*, GAO-08-554 (Washington, D.C.: June 16, 2008).

[20] The Bureau has procedures in place to remove duplications at a later date.

[21] Department of Commerce, Office of Inspector General, *2010 Census: Quarterly Report to Congress*, Final Report No. OIG-197914 (May 2010).

[22] GAO, *2000 Census: Actions Taken to Improve the Be Counted and Questionnaire Assistance Center Programs*, GAO/GGD-00-47 (Washington, D.C.: Feb. 25, 2000).

[23] The Bureau opened Be Counted sites on February 26, 2010, in areas where Bureau staff were hand delivering questionnaires to housing units with mostly rural route and PO Box addresses.

[24] QAC representatives at 23 of 43 sites did not comment on the level of activity at their sites. Of the 51 Be Counted/QAC sites visited, 43 were QAC-only sites and 8 were Be Counted-only sites.

In: The 2010 Census: Operations and Outcomes   ISBN: 978-1-61324-348-0
Editors: K. De Luca and C. Moretti   © 2011 Nova Science Publishers, Inc.

Chapter 4

2010 CENSUS: FOLLOW-UP SHOULD REDUCE COVERAGE ERRORS, BUT EFFECTS ON DEMOGRAPHIC GROUPS NEED TO BE DETERMINED[*]

United States Government Accountability Office

WHY GAO DID THIS STUDY

The U.S. Census Bureau (Bureau) puts forth tremendous effort to conduct a complete and accurate count of the nation's population and housing; yet some degree of error in the form of persons missed, duplicated, or counted in the wrong place is inevitable due to the complexity in counting a large and diverse population. The Bureau designed two operations, Coverage Follow-up (CFU) and Field Verification (FV), to reduce certain types of counting, or coverage, errors in the 2010 Census. GAO was asked to assess (1) the extent to which the Bureau completed CFU and FV on schedule and within estimated cost and (2) the implications of their key design elements for improving coverage.

GAO reviewed Bureau evaluations, planning, and other documents on CFU and FV, and prior GAO work, and interviewed Bureau officials.

---

[*] This is an edited, reformatted and augmented version of United States Government Accountability Office publication GAO-11-154, dated December 2010.

WHAT GAO RECOMMENDS

GAO recommends that the Secretary of Commerce direct the Bureau to assess (1) how well questions to help identify miscounted people on census forms helped reduce differences in the undercounts between demographic groups; (2) the degree to which telephone numbers led to completed contacts for households of various demographic characteristics; and (3) how trends in telecommunication usage and new technology may influence the effectiveness of CFU. The Secretary of Commerce concurred with our recommendations.

WHAT GAO FOUND

The Bureau completed CFU and FV on schedule and within budget. FV cost $21 million (about 38 percent less than estimated) and CFU cost about $267 million (about 2 percent less than estimated). These operations followed up on potential errors on census returns or lists of addresses after census data had been initially collected. Their completion provided follow-up data used by subsequent data processing that removed errors from the official census tabulations.

Three of the Bureau's key CFU design elements will likely improve overall census accuracy, but their effect on undercounts of different demographic groups is not clear. One key design element increased the number and types of follow-up cases. The Bureau expanded the scope of CFU from about 2 million households in the 2000 Census to more than 7 million in 2010. It also added 20 different types of households for potential follow-up. New types included households that reported members temporarily residing elsewhere, such as at college, in nursing homes, or in jail. According to the Bureau, the 2010 CFU operation should remove more than 2.7 million coverage errors from the census.

Another key design element of CFU prioritized follow-up cases based on their likelihood to result in a census correction, which was a reasonable attempt to leverage the resources for the operation. However, the Bureau's evaluation plans, based on considerations of what may best reduce cost or increase accuracy in the future, do not link the demographic characteristics of households to how they responded to the additional questions or CFU results for those households. Therefore, it is unclear whether the prioritized follow-up will help reduce differences in the accuracy of census counts across demographic groups.

Finally, CFU's design relied on a telephone-only approach to complete follow-up rather than personal visits. This limited costs, resulting in more follow-up and likely more coverage errors being removed from the census. But the telephone-only decision excluded about 700,000 households from CFU that could not be contacted by telephone. Prior Bureau experience indicates that some historically undercounted groups were less likely to be reachable by telephone, and more recent independent research suggests that trends in telecommunication usage may also make it harder to reach some demographic groups this way in the future. Yet the Bureau's evaluation plans do not include an assessment of either the usefulness of the telephone numbers it collected in reaching specific groups or the effect of these trends. Greater understanding of how best to reach different groups as well as the influence of trends on the effectiveness of CFU could help to control costs while working to further reduce differential undercounts.

ABBREVIATIONS

Bureau	U.S. Census Bureau
CFU	Coverage Follow-up
FV	Field Verification
IT	information technology

The U.S. Census Bureau (Bureau) puts forth tremendous effort to conduct a complete and accurate count of the nation's population and housing; nonetheless, some degree of error in the form of persons missed, duplicated, or counted in the wrong place during the decennial census is inevitable due to the complexity of counting a large and diverse population.

The Bureau estimates that the 2000 Census undercounted certain population groups, including minorities, renters, and children, but somewhat overcounted the population as a whole. An undercount occurs when the census misses an individual who should have been enumerated; an overcount occurs when an individual is counted in error. Differences among undercounts of ethnic, racial, and other groups are referred to as "differential undercounts," which may have implications for political representation and other uses of census data. In an effort to improve accuracy and reduce differential undercounts of the population in 2010, the Bureau conducted the Coverage

Follow-up (CFU) and Field Verification (FV) operations, two programs intended to clean up possible errors identified after households provided their census responses. During CFU, a contractor telephoned certain households in an attempt to determine if someone had been miscounted, such as when the number of people reported living in a household did not match the number of people whose name and demographic information was included on the household's census form. During FV, the Bureau visited addresses that had been provided by persons that thought they had been missed by the census and that did not match the Bureau's master address list. From the 2000 Census, the Bureau expanded CFU and allocated more than $200 million in additional funds—including $30 million provided by the American Recovery and Reinvestment Act of 2009[1]—which allowed the Bureau to include an additional 1.1 million households within the scope of CFU.

After reviewing the status of CFU in 2008, we recommended that the Bureau submit its plans for CFU to Congress and decide how it would conduct the operation.[2] The Bureau did so and completed CFU in August 2010 and FV in September 2010. As requested, for this review we examined (1) the extent to which FV and CFU were completed on schedule and within cost estimates, and (2) key design elements of CFU and FV, the implications for those design elements on improving coverage, and possible lessons learned to the extent similar efforts are used in the 2020 Census. This report is one of three we are releasing today.[3] The other reports focus on the Bureau's efforts to reach out to and enumerate hardto-count populations, and efforts to complete other key census-taking activities. Both reports identify preliminary lessons learned, as well as potential focus areas for improvement.

To meet both objectives, we assessed Bureau planning, testing, and schedule documents and interviewed Bureau officials to supplement and verify the currency and relevance of documentation obtained. For the first objective we also assessed the performance of CFU and FV against the cost, timeliness, and other metrics the Bureau used to monitor the operations. Additionally, for the second objective we reviewed our past reports and Bureau literature on known limitations of follow-up methods to identify key design elements and their implications. We also assessed Bureau study and evaluation plans. We conducted this performance audit from March 2010 to December 2010 in accordance with generally accepted government auditing standards. Those standards require that we plan and perform the audit to obtain sufficient, appropriate evidence to provide a reasonable basis for our findings and conclusions based on our audit objectives. We believe that the evidence obtained provides a reasonable basis for our findings and conclusions based on our audit objectives.

BACKGROUND

To help ensure a complete count, the Bureau had a number of operations aimed at capturing census data from people and households that otherwise might have been missed by the census. For example, the Be Counted program was designed to make special census questionnaires available to those who may not have received one, including people who do not have a usual residence, such as transients, migrants, and seasonal farm workers. The questionnaires were placed in over 38,000 locations across the country, including libraries, convenience stores, and other places people might frequent. The Bureau conducted FV to verify the existence of new addresses provided on these questionnaires and through other sources that were not already on the Bureau's master address list. The procedures enumerators followed to verify addresses in 2010 were largely similar to those used in the 2000 Census. In 2000, the Bureau visited nearly 900,000 addresses as part of its FV operation, verifying the addition of over 450,000 addresses to its address list.

To help ensure accuracy in the population count in 2000, the Bureau used telephone interviews in another operation to follow up with two types of household responses: households too large to include all their members on the form and households with apparent discrepancies on their questionnaires, such as when the number of people reported in the household population box does not match the number of people whose name and demographic information is included on the form. The Bureau placed calls to these households to determine if additional persons might have been missed (undercounted), if persons might have been counted in error (overcounted), or if persons might have been counted in the wrong place (possibly an overcount in one place and an undercount in another). The Bureau followed up on over 2.5 million households at a cost of approximately $67 million, resulting in over 152,000 people being added to the official census count and approximately 258,000 others being removed.

In response to Census 2000 experiences and in order to help achieve a Bureau goal of reducing differential undercounts, the Bureau added questions to the 2010 Census questionnaire to better identify potential coverage problems. These additional questions—called coverage probes— were to help identify households that may have omitted (undercounted) persons, due to familial relationships such as young children and extended family residing in the household but not reported on the census questionnaire due to space limitations, or households that may have counted persons more than once (overcounted), due to situations where members spent time elsewhere, such as relatives living in nursing homes or college dormitories. The resulting coverage probes used on the 2010 Census questionnaire are shown below in figure 1.

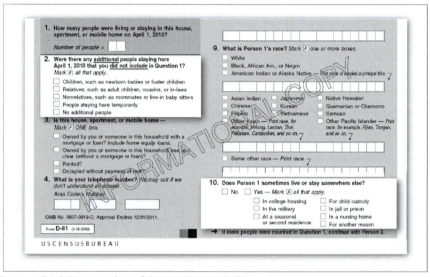

Source: GAO Presentation of Census Bureau Information.

Figure 1. The Bureau Used Probes on Census Questionnaires to Identify Households with Possible Coverage Errors.

THE BUREAU COMPLETED FV AND CFU ON SCHEDULE AND WITHIN BUDGET, BUT NEEDS TO IMPROVE THE ACCURACY OF ITS COST ESTIMATES

FV Was Completed on Schedule and Well under Budget

The 2010 FV operation began July 21, 15 days early, and finished on schedule on September 8, 2010. During that time, the Bureau visited nearly 456,000 addresses. The Bureau's preliminary results show that about 49 percent of those addresses were verified as valid housing units, 33 percent did not exist, and 18 percent were duplicates. The Bureau expects to report the final results in its formal evaluations of FV, planned for release in July 2011.

Completing FV on schedule was commendable, given that the Bureau had to make several late changes to the design of the operation as part of a contingency plan. Before beginning the FV operation, the information technology (IT) system the Bureau had expected to use to support the operation experienced testing and development delays. Furthermore, the Bureau was experiencing difficulty with this system being used to support other major census field operations. Therefore the Bureau developed and implemented a contingency plan, which substituted a modified version of the IT system used to support the 2010 Census Coverage Measurement operations and the IT system used for the 2000 Census, changed some related procedures for shipping workload materials, and significantly expanded the quality-assurance program to mitigate the risk of introducing additional changes to the contingency IT system. The Bureau attributes its ability to complete FV on time to its aggressive monitoring of the risk that IT systems might not be ready, its having identified a contingency IT system in advance, and the small scale of the FV operation compared to other census field operations, which allowed for the rapid adoption of alternative procedures. The Bureau's timely response to IT system delays demonstrates the benefits of the Bureau having developed risk mitigation plans for significant risks, as we have recommended before.[4]

The Bureau completed FV at a cost of $21 million, 38 percent lower than the $33.8 million estimated for the operation. Bureau officials are still researching why costs were lower than expected, but their preliminary analysis attributes cost savings to increased productivity and reduced operational inputs, such as training hours and mileage. The final cost of the operation was unexpected considering that the Bureau estimated that the late changes made by the contingency plan would increase the cost per case and increase total costs by nearly $15 million for the estimated workload. Under the Bureau's original calculation, adding the contingency plan raised the estimated cost-per-case to about $74, far more than the $53 per case assumed in the initial budget estimate or the $46 per case reported at the end of the operation. The Bureau has not attempted to separately identify how much of the final cost per case increase was attributable to the contingency plan or other factors.

Achieving cost savings is a positive development. However, our prior work has highlighted the need for the Bureau to develop more accurate and rigorous cost estimates for census operations.[5] A high-quality cost estimate is the foundation of a good budget, providing an estimate of the funding required to efficiently execute a program. Additionally, according to our *Cost Assessment Guide*, a cost estimate should be a "living" document that is continually updated as actual costs begin to replace original estimates, so that it remains relevant and current.[6] We have previously recommended[7] that the Bureau document where actual costs differ from those estimated to help document lessons learned and the basis for changes made to assumptions used. The Bureau updated its cost estimate for FV as its estimated workload changed and when it considered adoption of the contingency plan. However, moving forward it will be important to be able to explain the variation in its cost estimates.

CFU Was Completed on Schedule and Exceeded Performance Targets

The 2010 CFU operation began and finished on schedule, ensuring that CFU data were available for subsequent data processing. From April 11 to August 14, Bureau contractors telephoned nearly 7.4 million households, of which 4.9 million (66 percent) were complete interviews, meeting their estimated workload target. The Bureau expects to be able to report an analysis of the effect of CFU on census coverage in the spring of 2011.

The Bureau completed CFU at an estimated cost of $267 million, about 2 percent less than the initial cost estimate for the operation. As shown in table 1 below, the Bureau completed a slightly higher percentage of cases it attempted and spent on average less time on the phone completing each interview than expected.

Table 1. CFU Performance Exceeded Targets

Performance measure	Target	Actual
Case-completion rate (percent)	65	66
Cases completed per hour per interviewer	2.36	2.35
Average interviewer score for quality assurance (percent)	97	99
Average call time (seconds)	249	208

Source: Census Bureau.
Note: Data are from Census Bureau management reporting.

Given mandated deadlines that the Bureau faces for delivering census tabulations, completing field data collection including CFU and FV on schedule was crucial for subsequent processing activities to proceed and be completed on schedule.

CFU SHOULD HELP IMPROVE OVERALL CENSUS COVERAGE, BUT ITS EFFECT ON DIFFERENT DEMOGRAPHIC GROUPS MAY NOT BE UNIFORM

Three design decisions for the 2010 CFU operation should improve overall census accuracy. These decisions include

- expanding the scope of the 2010 CFU operation compared to its 2000 operation,
- prioritizing types of follow-up cases, and
- contacting identified CFU households using only the telephone.

The Bureau's Increase in the Number and Types of CFU Cases Should Improve Overall Census Accuracy

A key design decision the Bureau made for the 2010 CFU was to expand the scope of its coverage follow-up operation from 2000 to follow up on additional types of cases that it believed would help reduce the differential undercount. While continuing to follow up on the two types of cases that constituted the 2000 follow-up operation—large households and those with apparent count discrepancies—the Bureau identified 20 additional types of cases potentially to cover in 2010. One of these types of cases came from the use of administrative records from other federal sources, such as demographic information and addresses of families receiving tenant subsidies from an information system at the Department of Housing and Urban Development, to identify persons associated with a household's address who might have been omitted from the household's census form. Most of the additional types of cases were identified from responses to the new coverage probes on the census questionnaire discussed earlier. Additional types included households with responses indicating household members present who may not have been recorded on the initial census form, such as newborn babies, foster children, roommates or live-in babysitters, or household members who may have lived or stayed at more than one place, such as college students or nursing-home residents.

Expanding the scope of the 2010 CFU increased the number of cases the Bureau followed up on from about 2.5 million cases in 2000 to about 8 million cases in 2010. According to the Bureau, the 2010 CFU operation should result in more than 2.9 million coverage errors being removed from the census, including overcounts and undercounts, compared to more than 400,000 coverage errors being removed in 2000. The more coverage errors are removed from the official census count, the more the overall accuracy of the census is improved.

The Effect of the Bureau's Prioritization of Coverage Follow-up on Differential Undercounts Is Not Clear

A second key design decision the Bureau made for CFU was to prioritize the types of cases it would follow up on, likely increasing the overall number of coverage errors corrected but possibly affecting demographic groups differently. The Bureau had to prioritize follow-up cases, since the expansion of the CFU scope resulted in an estimated 22.5 million potential CFU cases, far exceeding what its time and budget for the 2010 CFU operation would permit. Bureau planning documents indicate that along with the extra time needed to pursue 22.5 million cases, it would have cost approximately $800 million more to complete all of the possible follow-up cases.

In April 2010, the Bureau formally documented its decision to prioritize follow-up based on cost and estimates of the number of corrections that would result from each type of case, and documented which cases it planned to include in follow-up. The Bureau estimated that in addition to households with apparent discrepancies on their questionnaires and households too large to include all their members on the form—the two types of cases it focused on in 2000—it would complete follow-up on 8 of 20 additional types of cases. However, due to a combination of higher call efficiency and lower-than-expected workloads for some of the selected types of cases, in the end the Bureau was able to follow up on an additional three types of CFU cases.

The Bureau's decisions to expand the scope of CFU and prioritize the CFU cases will likely result in a greater number of coverage errors being removed from official census tabulations than were removed in 2000, increasing CFU's effectiveness in improving overall census accuracy in 2010.

Prioritization of the CFU cases to contact was a reasonable attempt to leverage the resources and time available for the operation. However, because the specific coverage probes the Bureau used on census questionnaires do not clearly map to specific demographic groups, the extent to which the prioritized follow-up will help achieve the Bureau's goal of reducing the differential undercount is unclear. For example, one of the Bureau's priorities for follow-up was households indicating that persons may have been included who should have been counted elsewhere, such as persons in jail, in college, or in the military. Among the types that the Bureau did not follow up on were households that reported persons who were sometimes living elsewhere seasonally or as part of custody-sharing arrangements. The demographic characteristics of the people covered by each of these probes are not likely to be the same as the general population. Thus, following up on one set of cases but not others will likely have a different, though unknown, effect on particular demographic groups.

The Bureau acknowledges that, in so far as households in certain groups are not contacted by telephone but have coverage errors, there would likely be a smaller improvement in coverage for those demographic groups. Yet Bureau officials maintain that since it would be difficult to design follow-up based directly on household characteristics such as race and Hispanic origin, relying on situation- and relationship-based probes on census questionnaires—such as the Bureau did in 2010—may be the most effective way to identify coverage follow-up cases. To that end, the Bureau has 2010 data on how each household responded to each coverage probe and the demographics of each household, and will ultimately know which probes led to corrections of census coverage errors. The Bureau plans to report the demographic groups for which CFU identified corrections as part of its formal assessment of CFU, but that assessment does not include a link between the results for each probe and historically undercounted groups. Bureau officials have explained that its evaluation choices are driven by consideration of the best value to the decennial census in terms of informing possible cost benefit analyses and improvements to accuracy, and can change in response to new information the Bureau may obtain. Linking these data from 2010 CFU could help the Bureau decide which of the probes and priorities best helped the Bureau both improve overall accuracy and reduce the differential undercount, and better inform the Bureau decision making on the use of coverage probes for 2020.

The Effect of the Bureau's Telephone-Only Approach on Differential Undercounts Is Not Clear

A third key design decision the Bureau made for CFU was to rely solely on telephone interviews rather than use personal visits to contact households during the 2010 CFU operation. For those households the Bureau can reach by telephone, this decision should have enabled the Bureau to reduce many more census errors, because it allowed the Bureau to follow up with more households than it could have with personal visits using the same level of funding. A Bureau evaluation of its 2000 coverage follow-up activities suggested that personal visits be used for households for which the Bureau has no valid telephone number, noting that traditionally undercounted groups, such as renters and certain minority groups, were less likely to have valid phone numbers. Yet personal visits are significantly more expensive than telephone calls, costing about $71 per case compared to about $19 per case for telephone calls, according to Bureau results from a 2006 census test of CFU.

To increase the effectiveness of its telephone-only approach, the Bureau implemented several specific recommendations from its evaluation of the 2000 follow-up operation, including the use of a commercial database to assist with identifying the telephone numbers that were invalid or missing for CFU cases. Bureau officials believe that adopting these recommendations led to significant increases in the effectiveness of telephone follow-up, with reported response rates to telephone calls conducted as part of 2010 Census tests of 63 percent in 2004, 80 percent in 2005, and 78 percent in 2006. For 2010 CFU, Bureau management reporting indicates that the response rate exceeded its target goal of 65 percent.

The Bureau's decision to rely solely on telephone calls and related measures to complete CFU resulted in lower cost and more effective follow-up, and should contribute to a greater number of coverage errors being removed from official census tabulations compared to 2000. While these design decisions helped increase overall census accuracy, their effect on the Bureau's goal to reduce the differential undercount is less clear. This is because the Bureau excluded from CFU any household for which it did not obtain a useable telephone number. A useable phone number was obtained either from the respondent's return and could be a wireless or landline telephone number or through a telephone number look-up that resulted in the retrieval of landline numbers only. This is potentially problematic for two reasons.

First, current research indicates that there are significant differences between households that use only wireless telephones and those that have landline telephones, with groups of households with high wireless-only usage being part of historically undercounted populations.[8] According to our analysis of Bureau management reporting, the Bureau excluded about 700,000 households from follow-up because it lacked a usable contact telephone number. The Bureau relied only on landline telephone numbers from its commercial database, due to concerns about not knowing the geographic location of wireless phones it might dial and the possible financial burden on wireless customers from unsolicited calls. The Bureau did not immediately know which household-provided numbers were wireless, so it had rules concerning when calls could be made, to restrict calls to local times appropriate for the location of addresses provided. The Bureau has not attempted to track how many of the telephone numbers it called or excluded from follow-up were wireless numbers, what types of CFU cases they were for, or what the demographic characteristics of these households might be. According to the Bureau, it has asked the contractor that carried out the telephone calls for the Bureau to report the disposition of cases where a number was found during look-up as part of the contractor's forthcoming assessment. Future Bureau decisions about how to contact households for follow-up can be better informed if the Bureau strengthens its understanding of how different sources of contact information can affect its goal to reduce the differential undercount.

Furthermore, trends regarding the use of wireless telephones indicate that some households within hard-to-count populations may be harder to contact in the future using landline telephone operations. For example, a recent Centers for Disease Control and Prevention study shows that wireless-only households has more than doubled between January 2006 and December 2009 from about 11 percent to more than 24 percent of the nation's households. And in May 2010, the Pew Research Center found that wireless-only adults pose a significant challenge to data collection by telephone, because such adults are substantially different demographically from those reached on a landline phone. According to the Pew Research Center, wireless-only adults tend to be young, single, renters, and with lower income. This research also found that minorities made up a larger share of the wireless-only group with far more Hispanics, African-Americans, and people of other or mixed racial backgrounds than those with landline telephones. Such trends could pose a challenge to possible future Bureau reliance on telephone-based contacts intended to help improve census coverage of such demographic groups to the extent they do not provide their telephone numbers on census questionnaires. Broader ongoing shifts in the use of other telecommunications, including a variety of social media, may also influence the relative effectiveness of strategies relying on telephone communication.

CONCLUSIONS

Overall, the Bureau generally implemented FV and CFU on schedule and under budget, which is a noteworthy accomplishment given the inherent challenges of conducting a cost-effective census. The Bureau also updated its cost estimates for FV periodically as its estimated workload for FV evolved, and adopted design changes for CFU that likely contributed significantly to improving the overall accuracy of the census. At the same time, the Bureau's experience in implementing these two operations highlights additional actions that may improve the Bureau's understanding of the effectiveness of CFU in reducing differential undercounts and help improve planning for 2020 to the extent that the Bureau conducts such operations as part of the next decennial.

First, our previous work has highlighted the importance of accurate and rigorous cost estimates; thus, it will be important for the Bureau to assess the factors that led to significant variance in cost estimates for FV. Knowing this will allow the Bureau to develop more accurate cost estimates in the future, and will help the Bureau focus on cost containment as it prepares for the 2020 Census. We are not making recommendations at this time regarding the Bureau's cost estimation methods, as we have already done so in a previous report.[9] The Bureau agreed with those recommendations at that time and has begun implementing them.

Second, given the research and testing of coverage probes leading up to their use in 2010, it will be important for the Bureau to assess the degree to which the coverage probes helped address the differential undercount. This will help the Bureau understand whether the probes the Bureau prioritized for follow-up worked as intended and could help the Bureau determine which probes or other follow-up procedures to use in the future to improve census accuracy.

Third, it will be important for the Bureau to determine the effectiveness of the phone numbers it obtained from census returns or its commercial database in making contact with households of different follow-up and demographic groups. The decision to rely solely on telephone calls and no personal visits involved an implicit trade-off between the opportunity for cost savings with improved overall census accuracy and an opportunity possibly to help reduce historic differential undercounts. If the Bureau better understood the demographic composition of those for whom it did and did not obtain telephone numbers, and for whom it was and was not successful in reaching by phone, it could better determine the effect of this design decision on differential undercounts. Also, better knowledge of how best to reach different groups could help identify effective sources of contact information or strategies for using them for future censuses, further helping to control costs while still working to address differential undercounts.

Finally, whether it is a trend of households moving away from reliance on landlines, or other possible emerging trends related to growth in other modes of communication and new technology, the Bureau's future design decisions will benefit from tracking and assessing the implications of such trends and leveraging or mitigating their effect where possible. For example, under a scenario where the Bureau continues to rely on telephones for contacting households, the Bureau might need to adopt strategies for increasing the number of usable telephone numbers provided by census respondents or revisit its specific rules concerning when to dial numbers. Moving forward, it will be important for the Bureau to identify how rapid changes in technology and the public's use of them may affect the effectiveness of its efforts to improve census accuracy, both overall and in terms of reducing differential undercounts.

RECOMMENDATIONS FOR EXECUTIVE ACTION

We recommend that the Secretary of Commerce require the Director of the U.S. Census Bureau to take the following three actions to improve the Bureau's planning for the 2020 Census:

- To help the Bureau decide which coverage probes, if any, to use and prioritize for future follow-up efforts, assess the extent to which historically overcounted and undercounted demographic groups responded to the probes the Bureau followed up on and determine the effectiveness of specific probes in reducing differential undercounts.
- To support the Bureau's efforts to control costs while improving census accuracy, determine the demographic characteristics of the households for which it did and did not obtain telephone numbers and, to the extent feasible, assess the degree to which the telephone

numbers were usable and led to completed contacts for households of various follow-up groups and demographic characteristics.
- To ensure that the design of future follow-up efforts is effective in improving census coverage, assess the implications that trends in landline and wireless usage and other modes of communication and new technology may have both on the design decisions for future CFUlike operations and on their effectiveness in improving census coverage in terms of both overall census accuracy and differential undercounts.

AGENCY COMMENTS AND OUR EVALUATION

The Secretary of Commerce provided written comments on a draft of this report on December 1, 2010. The comments are reprinted in appendix I. The Department of Commerce agreed with the overall findings and recommendations and appreciated our efforts in helping the Bureau develop a successful evaluation plan for the 2020 Census. The department also included comments from the Bureau on certain statements in the report.

The Bureau commented on our discussion of its initial estimate that the contingency plan it adopted would increase the cost of FV. The Bureau commented that its initial estimate that the contingency plan would increase the cost of FV by $15 million was based on estimated workloads, that the final FV workload was much smaller, and that it had not attempted to reestimate the cost effect of the contingency plan separately. We revised the text to more fully reflect that the estimated increase was based on estimated workload, and emphasized the changes in "cost per case," which better reflects the effect on cost of changes in workload.

The Bureau also commented on our discussion of telecommunication trends and the Bureau's need to understand how different sources of contact information can affect its goal to reduce the differential undercount. The Bureau agreed that the trend toward wireless communication needs more attention in the future and described how it had not yet collected certain data that might be needed to carry out evaluation of the type we recommended. According to our analyses, the additional data are easily obtained. We revised the text to point more specifically to the type of data that could help the Bureau with future decisions about how to reach historically undercounted groups.

APPENDIX I: COMMENTS FROM THE DEPARTMENT OF COMMERCE

December 1, 2010

Mr. Robert Goldenkoff
Director
Strategic Issues
United States Government Accountability Office
Washington, DC 20548

Dear Mr. Goldenkoff:

The U.S. Department of Commerce appreciates the opportunity to comment on the draft report by the United States Government Accountability Office (GAO), entitled "2010 Census: Follow-up Should Reduce Coverage Errors, but Effects on Demographic Groups Need to be Determined" (GAO-11-154). The Department's comments on this report are enclosed.

Sincerely,

Gary Locke

Enclosure

U.S. Department of Commerce
Comments on the
United States Government Accountability Office
Draft Report, Entitled
"2010 Census: Follow-up Should Reduce Coverage Errors, but Effects on
Demographic Groups Need to be Determined"
(GAO-11-154)
December 2010

The U.S. Department of Commerce thanks the U.S. Government Accountability Office (GAO) for its efforts in examining the 2010 Census Coverage Follow-up (CFU) and Field Verification (FV) operations. The GAO assessed the Census Bureau's performance in completing these operations on schedule and within budget and evaluated their efficacy in accurately reducing coverage errors.

We have no fundamental disagreements with the overall findings or with the recommendations regarding items to be studied for the 2020 Census. However, the Census Bureau provides the following comments about statements and conclusions in this report.

- **Page 7, first full paragraph:** "The final cost of the operation was unexpected considering that the Bureau estimated that the late changes made by the contingency plan would increase costs by nearly $15 million."

  Census Bureau response: Prior to the operation, the Census Bureau used a preliminary workload estimate to roughly calculate operational costs under the contingency plan. Using the preliminary workload figures, the estimated impact was a $15 million increase in the budget. The actual workload was much lower than originally estimated. The total budget for the entire operation was only $33.8 million, including any impact of the contingency approach. The Census Bureau did not separate out the costs associated with the contingency plan, though clearly it would be less than the earlier $15 million estimate because the actual workload was much smaller than what was assumed when constructing that earlier impact estimate.

- **Page 16, paragraph continued from page 15:** "The Bureau has not attempted to track how many of the households it called or excluded from follow-up had wireless numbers, what types of CFU cases they were, or what the demographic characteristics of these households might be."

  Census Bureau response: The Census Bureau agrees the trend towards wireless numbers (and away from landlines) needs more attention in the future for operations like CFU that depend entirely on telephone interviews. Unfortunately, the Census Bureau did not collect the data during the 2010 Census CFU operation that would be needed to conduct the analysis GAO recommends. The numbers that we called during CFU came primarily from the telephone numbers that people provided to us on their 2010 Census questionnaire. Some of the numbers would have been for landline telephones, and some numbers would have been for wireless telephones. However, we didn't collect the information to know which numbers corresponded to which devices, or whether people we called on a landline telephone also had a wireless telephone number. For the 2020 Census research and testing program, the Census Bureau is committed to closely following and studying these trends towards wireless communications.

In conclusion, we acknowledge the GAO's extensive work in reviewing these activities, and we appreciate its ongoing efforts to help us develop a successful evaluation plan for the 2020 Census.

Note: Page numbers in the draft report may differ from those in this report.

End Notes

[1] Pub. L. No. 111-5, div. A, tit. II, 123 Stat. 115, 127.

[2] GAO, *2010 Census: Bureau Needs to Specify How It Will Assess Coverage Follow-up Techniques and When It Will Produce Coverage Measurement Results*, GAO-08-414 (Washington, D.C.: Apr. 15, 2008).

[3] GAO, *2010 Census: Key Efforts to Include Hard-to-Count Populations Went Generally as Planned; Improvements Could Make the Efforts More Effective for Next Census*, GAO-11-45 (Washington, D.C.: Dec. 14, 2010) and GAO, *2010 Census: Data Collection Operations Were Generally Completed as Planned, but Long-standing Challenges Suggest Need for Fundamental Reforms*, GAO-11-193 (Washington, D.C.: Dec. 14, 2010).

[4] GAO, *Information Technology: Census Bureau Needs to Improve Its Risk Management of Decennial Systems*, GAO-08-79 (Washington, D.C.: Oct. 5, 2007).

[5] GAO, *2010 Census: Census Bureau Should Take Acton to Improve the Credibility and Accuracy of Its Cost Estimate for the Decennial Census*, GAO-08-554 (Washington, D.C.: June 16, 2008).

[6] GAO, *GAO Cost Estimating and Assessment Guide: Best Practices for Developing and Managing Capital Program Costs*, GAO-09-3SP (Washington, D.C.: March 2009).

[7] GAO-08-554.

[8] National Center for Health Statistics, *Wireless Substitution: Early Release of Estimates from the National Health Interview Survey, July-December 2009* (May 2010). Pew Research Center, *Assessing the Cell Phone Challenge to Survey Research in 2010* (May 2010).

[9] GAO-08-554.

In: The 2010 Census: Operations and Outcomes ISBN: 978-1-61324-348-0
Editors: K. De Luca and C. Moretti © 2011 Nova Science Publishers, Inc.

Chapter 5

2010 CENSUS: COOPERATION WITH ENUMERATORS IS CRITICAL TO A SUCCESSFUL HEADCOUNT[*]

United States Government Accountability Office

WHY GAO DID THIS STUDY

On May 1, 2010, the U.S. Census Bureau (Bureau) will launch its massive follow-up effort with the roughly 48 million households that did not mail back their census forms (130 million forms were delivered). As part of this nonresponse follow-up effort, over 600,000 enumerators will fan out across the country, personally contacting nonresponding housing units as many as six times in an effort to ensure everyone is counted.

As requested, GAO's testimony in Los Angeles (L.A.) focuses on the importance of census participation, paying particular attention to (1) the Bureau's preparedness for nonresponse follow-up in terms of workload and staffing levels, (2) why it will be critical for Angelenos and others across the country to cooperate with enumerators during nonresponse follow-up, and (3) key steps the Bureau needs to take moving forward to ensure nonresponse follow-up is timely and accurate. The testimony is based on previously issued and ongoing GAO work.

---

[*] This is an edited, reformatted and augmented version of United States Government Accountability Office publication GAO-10-665T, dated April 30, 2010.

WHAT GAO RECOMMENDS

GAO is not making new recommendations in this testimony, but past reports recommended that the Bureau could build on lessons learned from 2000 to improve its 2010 nonresponse follow-up operation. The Bureau concurred with these recommendations and has taken steps to implement them.

WHAT GAO FOUND

Nationally, based on workload and staffing levels, the Bureau appears to be well positioned to implement nonresponse follow-up. On both counts, the Bureau's performance is meeting its expected goals. With respect to the mail-back response rate, the Bureau expected a level of between 59 percent and 65 percent. The actual mail-back response rate when the Bureau determined the universe of houses to visit for nonresponse follow-up on April 19, was 63.2 percent, well within its estimates. The mail-back response rate for L.A. City was 61.4 percent, and L.A. County was 64.7 percent. In terms of staffing, the Bureau met its goals both nationally as well as for L.A. Still, the Bureau could encounter pockets of challenges at the local level where mail-back response rates are less than expected. Further, the reliability of a computer system needed to administer nonresponse follow-up is an open question.

Participation in the census has decade-long implications for individuals, communities, and states. For example, census data are used to apportion House seats, redraw the boundaries of congressional and local election districts, and help ensure compliance with civil rights and other laws protecting our citizens. A complete count also helps ensure that L.A. and other areas obtain their fair share of federal assistance. Indeed, a number of formula grants allocate money based at least in part on census and related population data. GAO's recent analysis found that the 10 largest federal assistance programs obligated an estimated $478 billion in fiscal year 2009 based, to some extent, on census and related population data. The grants included Medicaid, Highway Planning and Construction, Head Start, and the Children's Health Insurance Program. Local governments as well as businesses use census data for planning and investment decisions, and to better tailor the services they provide.

Nationally, following up on nonresponding households is a daunting task, and L.A. presents its own challenges and opportunities. For example, data from a planning database the Bureau developed placed L.A. County first on a list of the top 50 U.S. counties with the highest number of people living in hard-to-count areas, based on data from the 2000 Census. Factors contributing to the area's hard-to-count challenges include poverty, unemployment, and language barriers. Moving forward, among other activities, it will be important for the Bureau to track various production, quality, and other indicators as planned to help ensure nonresponse follow-up stays on track.

In summary, participation in the census is a quick, easy, and confidential civic act that has a lasting impact on states, cities, neighborhoods, and even individuals. But the benefits that can accrue from a complete and accurate population tally can only occur if Angelenos cooperate with enumerators when they knock on nonrespondents' doors in the weeks ahead.

Mr. Chairman and Members of the Subcommittee:

I am pleased to be here today at the Center for Healthy Communities in Los Angeles (L.A.), to discuss the importance of participating in the 2010 Census. As you know, the U.S. Census Bureau (Bureau) goes to great lengths to secure a complete and accurate enumeration of the more than 300 million people that live in our country. In fact, the decennial census is an enterprise that few, if any, peacetime endeavors can match in terms of its size, scope, complexity, and fixed deadlines.

For the 2010 Census, the Bureau needed to successfully print 360 million questionnaires, hire a million temporary employees, partner with over 200,000 public and private sector entities across the country, and align thousands of disparate activities. The Bureau needs to do all of this and more, do it right, and do it under an extremely tight schedule. Perhaps most importantly, however, the Bureau cannot do it alone. To the contrary, participation in the census, just like voting and jury duty, is a civic responsibility that helps sustain a democratic society. What does this mean, exactly? After all, the census is fundamentally a head count. Does the participation of any one person really make a difference?

For Angelenos, as with people across the country, a complete count has implications for political representation and getting their fair share of federal assistance. This is because data from the census—a constitutionally mandated effort—are used to apportion seats in Congress, redraw congressional districts, help allocate more than $400 billion in federal aid to state and local governments each year, and remake local political boundaries. Census data are also used for planning purposes by the public and private sectors. The bottom line is that everything from House seats, to housing assistance, to investment decisions by L.A. businesses are determined, in whole or in part, by census data.

This afternoon's hearing is particularly timely as tomorrow the Bureau will launch its massive follow-up effort with the roughly 48 million households that did not mail back their census forms. As you know, the Bureau mailed out census questionnaires to around 120 million households in mid-March and hand delivered an additional 12 million questionnaires, mainly in rural areas, as well as in areas along the Gulf Coast affected by recent hurricanes. Both types of forms were to be returned by mail. On May 1, the Bureau's nonresponse follow-up operation begins. As part of the operation, over 600,000 enumerators will fan out across the country, personally contacting each nonresponding housing unit as many as six times in an effort to ensure everyone is counted.

Cooperation with census enumerators during this next phase of data collection will be especially important. The city of L.A.'s mail-back response rate as of April 19, 2010, when the Bureau determined the nonresponse follow-up workload, was 61.4 percent[1] (nationally, the mail-back response rate was just over 63 percent). During the 2000 Census, the city's mail-back response rate when it determined its nonresponse follow-up workload was 62.8 percent (the national mail-back response rate for the short form, at that time, was 66.4 percent).[2] For those who did not mail back their census forms, nonresponse follow-up will be the last opportunity to be directly counted in the census.

As requested, my remarks today will focus on the importance of census participation, paying particular attention to (1) the Bureau's preparedness for nonresponse follow-up in terms of workload and staffing levels, (2) why it will be critical for Angelenos and others across the country to cooperate with enumerators during nonresponse follow-up, and (3) key steps the Bureau needs to take moving forward to ensure nonresponse follow-up is timely and accurate.

My testimony today is based on our ongoing and completed reviews of key census-taking operations (see "Related GAO Products" at the end of this statement). In these reviews we analyzed key documents—including plans, procedures, and guidance for the selected activities—and interviewed cognizant Bureau officials at headquarters and local census offices. In addition, we made on-site observations of certain census activities across the country. These observations included the Bureau's nonresponse follow-up efforts during the 2000 Census in various locations across the country, among them three sections of L.A.: Hollywood/Mid-Wilshire, L.A. Downtown, and

Santa Monica. For the 2010 Census, we observed key census-taking activities in L.A., as well as in Fresno and San Bernardino, California; plus Atlanta, Georgia; Philadelphia, Pennsylvania; and Washington, D.C., among other locations. We selected these cities because of their geographic and demographic diversity, among other factors. Further, to gain greater insight into the local census operations, we surveyed the Bureau's 494 local census office managers using a series of online questionnaires about their experience in managing local census office activities.

On April 19, 2010, we provided the Bureau with a statement of facts for our audit work, and on April 22, 2010, the Bureau provided technical comments, which we included as appropriate. We conducted our work in accordance with generally accepted government auditing standards. Those standards require that we plan and perform the audits to obtain sufficient, appropriate evidence to provide a reasonable basis for our findings and conclusions based on our audit objectives. We believe that the evidence obtained provides a reasonable basis for our findings and conclusions based on our audit objectives.

BACKGROUND

The Bureau takes extraordinary measures to produce a complete and accurate census. To date, for example, the Bureau has sent questionnaires to 120 million housing units for occupants to complete and mail back. The Bureau also hand-delivered around 12 million questionnaires—mostly in rural areas as well as in areas along the Gulf Coast affected by recent hurricanes—for residents to fill out and return via mail. In March and April, the Bureau simultaneously launched operations aimed at counting people in migrant worker housing, boats, tent cities, homeless shelters, nursing homes, dormitories, prisons, and other diverse dwellings, all in an effort to secure a complete count.

For those individuals who do not mail back their census forms, the Bureau attempts to include them through its nonresponse follow-up operation, which is scheduled to run from May 1 through July 10. During this operation, over 600,000 enumerators are to go door-to-door collecting census information from each address from which a questionnaire was not received. Nonresponse follow-up is the most costly and labor-intensive of all census-taking operations. The Bureau expects nonresponse follow-up will cost around $2.3 billion, or around 16 percent of the decennial's total estimated lifecycle cost of around $14.7 billion. By comparison, according to Bureau data on the 2000 nonresponse follow-up operation, labor, mileage, and certain administrative costs alone amounted to around $1.76 billion (in 2010 dollars), or about 22 percent of the total $8.15 billion (in 2010 dollars) lifecycle cost of the 2000 Census.

Importantly, nonresponse follow-up is the last opportunity for people to be directly counted in the census. Those individuals who are missed by, or who do not respond to, census enumerators, are included through methods that are indirect and not as accurate. In cases of refusal, enumerators may be instructed to try to find a proxy respondent who might know something about the occupants of a household. If this is infeasible, data on the household are statistically imputed based on the demographic characteristics of surrounding housing units.

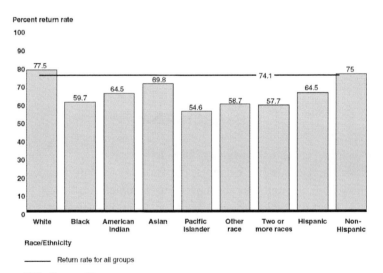

Source: U.S. Census Bureau.

Figure 1. Mail Return Rates by Race/Ethnic Groups during the 2000 Census.

This is significant for Angelenos for two reasons. First, for 2010, the mail-back response rate, used for determining the nonresponse follow-up workload, of 61.4 percent for the city of L.A. is lagging the national rate of 63.2 percent. Second, in 2000, minority groups, which comprise a large share of L.A.'s population, tended to return their questionnaires at a lower rate compared to other groups, and were more likely to be missed by the census. For example, as shown in figure 1, nationally in 2000, whites had a higher mail return rate

(77.5 percent) than the rate for all groups (74.1 percent), while nearly every other race/ethnic group had lower return rates than the total mail return rate.[3] The lowest mail return rates were those of Pacific Islander (54.6 percent) and multi-racial (57.7 percent) households. Participating in nonresponse follow-up represents an important opportunity to improve the quality of census data.

Despite these elaborate efforts to obtain a complete count, some amount of error is unavoidable. However, what makes these errors particularly problematic is their differential impact on various subgroups. Minorities, renters, and children, for example, are more likely to be missed by the census while more affluent groups, such as people with vacation homes, are more likely to be included more than once.

The Bureau Is Positioned to Conduct Nonresponse Follow-up but Could Encounter Local and Other Challenges

Nationally, in terms of workload (as measured by the mail-back response rate) and staffing levels, the Bureau appears to be well positioned to implement nonresponse follow-up. On both counts, the Bureau's performance is meeting its expected goals. Nevertheless, national-level data can mask challenges occurring at the local level, and there are areas throughout the country where either the mail-back response rate or staffing levels are lagging.

With respect to the mail-back response rate, the Bureau expected a level of between 59 percent and 65 percent. The actual mail-back response rate when the Bureau determined the universe of houses to visit for nonresponse follow-up on April 19, was just over 63 percent, well within its estimates.[4] This translates into a workload of around 48 million housing units. Achieving this mail-back response rate is an important accomplishment as the nation's population is growing steadily larger, more diverse, and according to the Bureau, increasingly difficult to find and reluctant to participate in the census.

High mail-back response rates are important because they save taxpayer dollars. According to the Bureau, for every one-percentage point increase in mail response in 2010, the Bureau saves $85 million that would otherwise have been spent on nonresponse follow-up. According to the Bureau, it costs 42 cents to mail back each census form in a postage-paid envelope, compared with $57 for census takers to visit each home. Moreover, mail returns tend to have better quality data.

Key factors aimed at improving the mail-back response rate included the mailing of a reminder postcard; sending a second or "replacement" questionnaire to around 30 million households in census tracts that had the lowest response rates in the 2000 Census, and 12-million replacement questionnaires to nonresponding households in other census tracts that had low-to-moderate response rates in 2000; and an aggressive marketing and outreach program.

The Bureau also appears to be in good shape nationally from the perspective of enumerator staffing. In terms of recruiting, the Bureau's goal was to recruit 3.7 million applicants to fill over 600,000 enumerator and other positions by April 25. As of April 11, the Bureau had recruited 3,717,757 applicants, or 101 percent of its target.

While the Bureau appears to be well-positioned from a national perspective to carry out nonresponse follow-up, the decennial is essentially a local endeavor, where the operational environment and challenges the Bureau faces vary markedly from one locale to another. In this regard, several locations stand out. For example, the mail-back response rates in some large cities trail the 2010 national response rate of 63.2 percent, and/or the response rate they achieved during the 2000 Census. They include Detroit, New Orleans, San Antonio, and San Diego (see table 1).

Table 1. Selected Cities with Mail-Back Response Rates for 2010 that Are Lower than 2000

City	City Mail-Back Response Rates (percent)		
	2000 Census	2010 Census (as of April 19, 2010)	Difference
Detroit	61.4	45.9	15.5
New Orleans	50.1	42.5	7.6
San Antonio	66.9	61.0	5.9
San Diego	71.5	64.5	7

Source: GAO analysis of U.S. Census Bureau data.

Likewise, there are three local census offices that have less than two qualified applicants per field position--the Bureau's recruitment target. These offices continue their recruiting efforts, and the Bureau has plans to staff operations with recruits from neighboring local census offices, if necessary.

With respect to L.A., as shown in table 2, L.A. City is trailing the state and national mail-back response rates as of April 19, 2010, as well as comparable benchmarks from the 2000 Census.

Table 2. 2010 Census Mail-Back Response Rates Compared to 2000

	Census Mail-Back Response Rates (percent)	
Level of Geography	2000 Census	2010 Census (as of April 19, 2010)
National	66.4	63.2
California	68.9	64.6
L.A. County	68.3	64.7
L.A. City	62.8	61.4

Source: GAO analysis of U.S. Census Bureau data.

In terms of recruiting, the L.A. region has met its recruiting goals. For example, the Bureau's recruiting goal for the L.A. region was 266,370, and as of April 18, 2010, the Bureau had recruited 350,187 or 131 percent of its goal. Starting pay for enumerators, which is based on local labor markets, is $17 per hour in the L.A. area.

Aside from workload and staffing, the reliability of the Bureau's automated systems, and in particular an information technology (IT) system used for managing the Bureau's field operations, is an open question. In earlier tests and prior activities, the operational control system did not function reliably, and the Bureau had to restrict the number of users in local census offices because of capacity limitations. The Bureau has taken steps to mitigate the risks posed by the unreliable IT systems, including upgrading hardware and software, but time will tell whether they will be able to perform as needed under full operational loads.

COOPERATION WITH ENUMERATORS WILL HELP CALIFORNIA COUNT IN THE 2010 CENSUS

Census Data Are Critical for Representative Democracy

The Constitution requires a census every 10 years in order to apportion seats in the House of Representatives. Moreover, while not required by the Constitution, states use census data to redraw the boundaries of congressional districts. Although a few missed households might not seem particularly problematic, especially in a nation of more than 300 million people, a complete count is necessary because, in some cases, small differences in population totals could potentially impact apportionment or redistricting decisions, or both. Indeed, during the 2000 Census, the last House seat could have gone to Utah rather than North Carolina if Utah's population had around 850 more people.

More broadly, census data are used to help protect our democratic system of government. For example, block-by-block census data were used in reapportioning state legislatures in the 1960s, as discussed in the Supreme Court's "one person, one vote" landmark case of Reynolds v. Sims.[5] Further, census data are used to help ensure compliance with federal civil rights and other laws protecting our citizens.

Census Data Are Used to Allocate Federal Aid to States and Localities

Many federal assistance programs are funded by formula grants that have historically relied, at least in part, on census and related population data to allocate funds. In our recent analysis, we found that the 10 largest federal assistance programs obligated an estimated $478 billion in fiscal year 2009 based, to some extent, on census and related population data.[6] This amount represents about 84 percent of total federal assistance. The grants included Medicaid, Highway Planning and Construction, Head Start, and the Children's Health Insurance Program.

A recent study by the Brookings Institution calculated that in fiscal year 2008, federal assistance programs distributed a total of $19.8 billion in total program expenditures, or $1,988 for each person in L.A. County.[7] Medicaid, a joint federal-state program that finances health care for certain low-income individuals, was by far the single largest program, accounting for $14.7 billion, or around 75 percent of total expenditures. Other assistance went to programs that included transportation, education, training, employment, social services, and income security.

Beyond these specific numbers, this much is clear: While population is one of several factors that can affect the distribution of federal assistance, boosting the participation rate, especially for hard-to-count groups, helps ensure that Angelenos obtain their fair share of federal assistance. This is a particularly important goal given the fiscal challenges that L.A. and the state of California are facing.

Local Governments Use Census Data to Plan for and Provide Services

The decennial census yields data that states use not only to determine boundaries for congressional districts, but also to establish boundaries for smaller jurisdictions such as local election and school districts. The census is also a rich source of data to help county and city governments plan for and provide a variety of services. For Angelenos, this could mean help in answering such questions as:

- Will the population of preschoolers in various neighborhoods warrant building additional elementary schools?
- Are the mass transit systems reaching the people likely to use public transport?
- Where and when should the next senior citizen facility be built?

Without federal census data, state and local governments would have to undertake their own headcounts, a costly alternative given the Census Bureau's experience and economies of scale. Further, a less-than-complete count could result in the inefficient allocation of taxpayer dollars.

Census Data Help Businesses Make Investment and Planning Decisions

Businesses use the aggregated census data to plan for and provide their services and goods. Census data about population trends help businesses succeed—and provide jobs in the process—by alerting them of opportunities to provide new services and products and to tailor existing ones to reflect demographic changes. Census data also help businesses efficiently target their advertising dollars and better meet the needs of their clients and customers. For example, a free issue of a magazine focused on the interests of Hispanic readers can be distributed based on information at the census block level. Likewise, retail chains can use census data to inform decisions on what mix of multicultural products—from cosmetics to music—they should carry. Companies also use population data to locate where to place new stores, as well as where to place production facilities where they can expect to find a suitable labor force.

Census Participation Is Safe

While the Bureau does a lot with the information people report, there are a number of things the Bureau will not do with it. For example, the answers that are provided cannot be shared with anyone, including law enforcement or tax collection agencies. The answers cannot be used in court, and they cannot be obtained with a Freedom of Information Act request. Federal law protects respondents' privacy and keeps the information confidential.

Further, in March 2010, the U.S. Justice Department confirmed that provisions of the Patriot Act[8] that pertain to the gathering and sharing of information do not override legal provisions that protect the confidentiality of census data. In short, everyone who lives in the country should feel safe about participating in the census, regardless of their immigration status.

KEY STEPS COULD HELP ENSURE TIMELY AND ACCURATE FOLLOW-UP OPERATIONS

Nationally, following up on nonresponding households is a daunting task, and L.A. presents its own challenges and opportunities. For example, data from a planning database the Bureau developed placed L.A. County first on a list of the top 50 U.S. counties with the highest number of people living in hard-to-count areas, based on data from the 2000 Census. Specifically, 4.4 million people of L.A. County's total population of more than 9 million people (46 percent) lived in hard-to-count census tracts in 2000. Factors contributing to the area's hard-tocount challenges include poverty, unemployment, and language barriers.

In our review of nonresponse follow-up during the 2000 Census, we noted that the Bureau has historically faced the combined challenge of (1) collecting quality data directly from household members, while (2) completing the operation on schedule, before error rates can increase as people move or have trouble remembering who was living at their homes on Census Day (April 1, 2010), as well as for keeping subsequent operations on track. For methodological reasons, the Bureau needs to complete its field data collection workload before a subsequent accuracy check can begin.[9]

During the 2000 Census, finding the optimal balance between these two objectives was sometimes a challenge for the Bureau. Indeed, to help ensure that local census offices completed nonresponse follow-up on schedule, the

Bureau developed ambitious interim "stretch" goals that called on local census offices to complete 80 percent of their nonresponse follow-up workload within the first 4 weeks of the operation and be completely finished by the end of the 8th week of the 10-week long effort. We found that these production goals generated mixed results.

Specifically, 17 percent of the sample of local census office managers we surveyed during the 2000 Census believed that the pressure had a positive or significantly positive impact; 41 percent believed that scheduling pressure had little or no impact on the quality of the operation; and 40 percent of the respondents believed that the pressure during nonresponse follow-up had a negative or significantly negative impact on the quality of the enumeration. Of those managers in the latter group, a common perception appeared to be that production was emphasized more than accuracy and that the schedule required local census offices to curtail procedures that could have improved data quality. Further, a small number of local census offices improperly collected less complete data and took other shortcuts (which the Bureau took steps to rectify).

Nationally, however, our analysis of Bureau data showed that those local census offices that completed their 2000 Census nonresponse follow-up workloads faster than the others did not collect larger quantities of less-than-complete data, such as partial interviews.

For the 2010 Census, the Bureau will conduct a quality assurance procedure it refers to as "outlier reinterviews," where the Bureau is to revisit or "reinterview" those households where characteristics of an enumerator's work differ from other enumerators collecting data in the same vicinity. In such cases, enumerators could be fabricating data. Outlier reinterviews are one of several types of reinterviews the Bureau plans to use for 2010.

Although the Bureau had procedures for various types of reinterviews, including a form of outlier reinterviews, for the 2000 Census, local census office managers often decided against conducting them. Indeed, 52 local census offices—about 10 percent of all local offices—did not conduct any reinterviews after a random check of enumerators' initial work. For the 2010 Census, the outlier interview cases will be automatically selected as opposed to being controlled by clerks in the local census offices. This could help ensure that outlier cases are investigated per the Bureau's reinterview procedures.

More generally, as the Bureau completes its nonresponse follow-up workload, it will be important for it to closely track various indicators of the pace, production levels, and quality of the operation as planned, and quickly investigate and appropriately address any peculiarities that could be indicative of falsification or other data quality issues. At the same time, it will be important for the Bureau to fully leverage its partnership program—an effort where specially trained Bureau employees engage key government and community organizations to support the census—to help pave the way for nonresponse follow-up and improve cooperation with enumerators. For example, based on our review of the 2000 Census, partnership staff could, among other activities, reach out to building managers and community leaders to gain access to secure apartment buildings and gated communities, and take other steps to deal with enumeration challenges.

However, the initial results of our 2010 survey on local census office managers suggest that there is room for improvement, in many cases, in the relationships between the local census offices and partnership staff. For example, of the 395 of 494 local census office managers who responded to our question about their satisfaction with the communication between the local census office and with partnership staff, 39 percent indicated they were generally or very satisfied, 46 percent were generally or very dissatisfied, and 14 percent were neither satisfied or dissatisfied.

Likewise, when asked about the partnership staff's assistance with local challenges, 39 percent of responding local census office managers were generally or very satisfied, 43 percent were generally or very dissatisfied, while 18 percent were neither satisfied nor dissatisfied.

The 26 local census office managers in the Bureau's L.A. region—an area extending from L.A. proper south to the Mexican border—held views similar to managers nationwide. Moving forward, it will be important for the Bureau to take appropriate steps to ensure that the efforts of the partnership staff are aligned with and fully supportive of the activities carried out by local census offices. For example, one partnership specialist we met with noted that having weekly, in-person meetings with local census office managers helped coordinate the work they were doing.

CONCLUDING OBSERVATIONS

As measured by workload and staffing levels, the Bureau is generally well-positioned to launch nonresponse follow-up. The operation starts tomorrow and will have more than 600,000 enumerators fan out across the country, collecting census information from those households that did not mail back their forms.

That said, the success of the enumeration is determined as much by what happens at the local level, as by national trends. With that in mind, the level of cooperation that occurs in the coming weeks on doorsteps across the country—as well as right here in downtown and South L.A.; Echo Park and Westlake; Wilshire and East Hollywood; and in neighborhoods all across L.A. City and County—will determine, to a large degree, the ultimate cost and quality of the decennial census.

Mr. Chairman and members of this Subcommittee, this concludes my statement. I would be happy to respond to any questions that you might have at this time.

End Notes

[1] The boundaries of the census tracts used to generate these estimates are not identical to the actual political boundaries of the city so the actual value for the city may differ slightly.

[2] In the 2000 Census, the Bureau mailed out both long- and short-form questionnaires. The short-form questionnaire had a higher response rate because it had fewer questions. For the 2010 Census, the Bureau used only a short-form questionnaire. For this testimony we use the 2000 Census short-form mail response rate when comparing 2000 and 2010 mail-back response rates.

[3] The mail return rate differs from the mail response rate in that the mail response rate is calculated as a percentage of all the housing units in the mail-back universe, including those that are later discovered to be nonexistent or unoccupied. The Bureau uses this mail-back response percentage as an indicator of its nonresponse follow-up workload.

[4] As discussed in the previous footnote, the mail-back response rate is calculated as a percentage of all forms in the mail-back universe from which the Bureau received a questionnaire. Although it includes households whose forms were returned by the U.S. Postal Service as "undeliverable" and thus might be vacant or nonexistent, the Bureau still sends enumerators to follow-up on them to ensure a complete count. We report the mail-back response rate because it is a measure of the nonresponse follow-up workload; the workload, in turn, has implications for the final cost of the census. On its Web site, the Bureau reports what it refers to as the "participation rate." This number differs from the mail-back response rate in that it excludes undeliverable questionnaires. The Bureau reports this figure because it is a better indicator of the public's cooperation with the census.

[5] 377 U.S. 533 (1964).

[6] GAO, *Formula Grants: Funding for the Largest Federal Assistance Programs Is Based on Census-Related Data and Other Factors,* GAO-10-263 (Washington, D.C.: Dec. 15, 2009).

[7] Andrew Reamer, *Counting for Dollars: The Role of the Decennial Census in the Distribution of Federal Funds,* Brookings (Washington, D.C.: March 2010).

[8] Pub. L. No. 107-56, 115 Stat. 272. The Patriot Act was enacted following the September 11, 2001, attacks in order to assist in the prevention of future terrorist incidents.

[9] GAO, *2000 Census: Best Practices and Lessons Learned for More Cost-Effective Nonresponse Follow-up,* GAO-02-196 (Washington, D.C.: Feb. 11, 2002).

In: The 2010 Census: Operations and Outcomes ISBN: 978-1-61324-348-0
Editors: K. De Luca and C. Moretti © 2011 Nova Science Publishers, Inc.

Chapter 6

2010 CENSUS: PLANS FOR CENSUS COVERAGE MEASUREMENT ARE ON TRACK, BUT ADDITIONAL STEPS WILL IMPROVE ITS USEFULNESS[*]

United States Government Accountability Office

WHY GAO DID THIS STUDY

Assessing the accuracy of the census is essential given that census data are used to apportion seats in Congress, to redraw congressional districts, and for many other public and private purposes. The U.S. Census Bureau's (Bureau) Census Coverage Measurement program (CCM) is to assess the accuracy of the 2010 Census and improve the design of operations for the 2020 Census. In April 2008, GAO recommended that the Bureau identify how it would relate CCM results—where the 2010 Census was accurate and inaccurate—to census operations to improve future censuses. Knowing where the 2010 Census was inaccurate can help inform research to improve the 2020 Census.

GAO was asked to examine (1) the status of CCM planning and (2) the effects of design decisions since GAO issued its April 2008 report. GAO

---

[*] This is an edited, reformatted and augmented version of United States Government Accountability Office publication GAO-10-324, dated April 2010.

reviewed Bureau documents related to CCM design and National Academy of Sciences reports, and interviewed responsible Bureau officials.

WHAT GAO RECOMMENDS

GAO is making recommendations to improve the Bureau's use of CCM in planning for future operations, with which the Department of Commerce generally agreed. Commerce stated that it is taking action to ensure data preservation. Further, Commerce stated that although it considers a 2000 contamination study comprehensive, a new recall bias study is planned for 2010.

WHAT GAO FOUND

Since GAO's April 2008 report, the Bureau has finalized plans for 2010 CCM goals, the timing of operations, and the types of results to be produced. Planning continues in other areas, such as developing estimation methods, evaluating the CCM program, and implementing its Master Trace Project, which would enable the Bureau to link its datasets and systems to support a broad range of research. The deadlines for some of these plans have not yet passed, but the Bureau already has default plans in place in case further changes do not occur. In mid-December, the Director decided to make some additional changes to the CCM program to improve the quality of CCM results.

GAO found that additional actions on Bureau decisions may make CCM more useful in informing Bureau decisions on future census and coverage measurement efforts:

- The Bureau's 2020 planning efforts are described in a series of decision memoranda issued in the summer of 2009. However, the Bureau has not yet taken steps to integrate CCM results with early 2020 planning to prepare for a census test in 2014. By describing, for example, what the Bureau might learn from CCM or how the results might feed into 2020 Census planning, the Bureau will better ensure that there are no gaps or overlaps in the use of CCM for early 2020 planning.

- In September 2009, the Bureau began its Master Trace Project, which is intended to ensure that its datasets and systems can be used together to support detailed research into the causes of census coverage problems and facilitate research on the possible interactions of future operations. At the time of this review, the Bureau had not yet completed an inventory of the census databases that might be of potential interest for future research, identified which archived versions might be most useful, or mapped out how they might be archived and linked. Doing this quickly will be important as the census is already underway and it will be difficult to make changes to database structures or archival and data storage plans if the Bureau's assessments determine that changes are necessary.
- The Bureau reviewed its previous decision to start CCM's Person Interviewing operation later than it did in 2000, and decided in June 2009 not to change it. However, the Bureau does not have a plan to assess the trade-offs in error between earlier and later start dates. Additional research on the trade-offs of different start dates could help the Bureau more fully understand the implications of CCM timing decisions on the resulting estimates of coverage error and better determine the optimal timing of Person Interviewing in future censuses.

Data from the decennial census—a constitutionally mandated count of the national population—are used to apportion seats in Congress, redraw congressional districts, allocate billions of dollars in federal assistance to state and local governments each year, and inform the planning and investment decisions of numerous public and private sector entities. The census aims to locate and count people—only once—in the right place, and collect complete and correct information about them. Because census data are central to so many critical functions, it is essential to assess census accuracy and improve the process when needed.

In April 2008, we reported that the U.S. Census Bureau (Bureau) needed to finalize plans for its Census Coverage Measurement (CCM) program—the effort intended to assess the accuracy of the 2010 Census and improve the design of operations for the 2020 Census—and made related recommendations to the Bureau's parent agency, the Department of Commerce.[1] In particular, we noted that the Bureau should produce plans that include (1) a description of when it will provide CCM results, (2) how it plans to report its CCM results in relation to census operations, and (3) key decision points and plans for evaluating aspects of the CCM. Commerce has taken steps to implement actions for each recommendation. Since we issued our report, the National Academy of Sciences panel on Correlation Bias and Coverage Measurement in the 2010 Decennial Census released its final report on the Bureau's plans for CCM,[2] recommending numerous steps to enhance the value of the program.

You asked us to examine the current plan for the CCM program and to provide (1) an update on the status of the planning since our April 2008 report, and (2) the potential effects of major CCM decisions on the quality and usefulness of CCM data. To meet these objectives, we reviewed Bureau documents related to CCM design and National Academy of Sciences (NAS) reports, and we interviewed Bureau officials responsible for CCM. We focused primarily on the Bureau's decisions in the following areas: 2010 CCM goals, timing of operations and reporting results, estimation methods, results to be produced, program evaluation, and implementing its Master Trace Project. Specifically, to update the status of CCM, we reviewed scheduling documents and decision memorandums. To identify the potential effects we reviewed decision memorandums and related justifications, prior Bureau and NAS research and our reports related to CCM and evaluation. We conducted our work from June 2009 to February 2010 in accordance with generally accepted government auditing standards. Those standards require that we plan and perform the audit to obtain sufficient, appropriate evidence to provide a reasonable basis for our findings and conclusions based on our audit objectives. We believe that the evidence obtained provides a reasonable basis for our findings and conclusions based on our audit objectives.

BACKGROUND

The Bureau puts forth tremendous effort to conduct a complete and accurate count of the nation's population; nonetheless, some degree of coverage error is inevitable because of the inherent complexity of counting the nation's large and diverse population and limitations in census-taking methods. These census coverage errors can take a variety of forms, including a person missed (an undercount), a person counted more than once (an overcount), or a person who should not have been counted, such as a child born after Census Day (another type of overcount). To further understand and to inform users about the quality of the census, the Bureau has been evaluating coverage measurement for more than 50 years. While initial evaluations relied solely on demographic analysis— population estimates based on birth and death rates as well as immigration estimates—modern coverage measurement began with the 1980 Census when the Bureau began also comparing census counts to survey results from an independent coverage measurement sample of the population. Using statistical methods, the Bureau generated detailed measures of the differences among undercounts of particular ethnic, racial, and other groups, which have been referred to as "differential undercounts." These measures were also generated for the 1990 and 2000 censuses.

Although the Bureau considered doing so in earlier decades, it has never used its estimates of coverage error to adjust census data. In 1980, the Director of the Census Bureau decided that potential adjustments would be flawed due to missing and inaccurate data. In 1990, the Bureau recommended statistically adjusting census data; however, the Secretary of Commerce determined that the evidence to support an adjustment was inconclusive and decided not to adjust. For the 2000 Census, a 1999 Supreme Court ruling held that the Census Act prohibited the use of statistical sampling to generate population data for apportioning the House of Representatives.[3] The Bureau had planned to produce apportionment numbers using traditional census-taking methods, and provide statistically adjusted numbers for non-apportionment uses of the data such as congressional redistricting and allocating federal funds. The Bureau later determined that its statistical estimates did not provide a reliable measure of census accuracy and could not be used to adjust the non-apportionment census data.

The Bureau is not planning to use CCM to adjust the 2010 Census. Instead, CCM will be used to evaluate coverage error to improve the 2020 and future censuses, and will focus on estimating various components of census coverage in addition to net coverage errors—the net effect on coverage after undercounts and overcounts are considered. These components of coverage include correct enumerations, erroneous enumerations (people or housing units that were counted but should not have been), and omissions (people or housing units that were not counted but should have been). The Bureau also plans to include imputations (counts of people and their characteristics that are provided for nonresponding households, usually based on responses from others under similar circumstances, such as from surrounding households).

Statistical measurements of census coverage are obtained by comparing and matching the housing units and people counted by the independent coverage measurement sample to those counted by the census in and around the sample areas. The Bureau has developed separate address lists—one for the entire nation of over 134 million housing units that it will use to conduct the census and one for coverage measurement sample areas—and will collect each set of data through independent operations. For the 2010 Census, census operations began collecting population data from households in January 2010 and will continue through the end of July, while CCM operations will collect data by visiting each of the housing units in the coverage measurement sample during an operation called Person Interviewing from August through October.

The statistical methodology the Bureau uses to estimate net coverage errors relies on an assumption that the chance that a person is counted by the census is not affected by whether he or she is counted in the independent coverage measurement sample, or vice versa. Because violating this "independence" assumption can bias coverage estimates, the Bureau takes special measures to maintain CCM's separation from the census, such as developing a separate address list for the coverage measurement sample discussed above.

THE BUREAU HAS FINALIZED DECISIONS IN SOME KEY AREAS SINCE OUR 2008 REPORT

Since our April 2008 report, the Bureau has finalized its plans in key areas of the CCM program including CCM's goals, the timing of operations, and the timing and types of results to be produced. Planning continues in other areas, such as developing estimation methods, evaluating the CCM program, and implementing its Master Trace Project. Continued progress and adherence to schedule will be important to ensure that the Bureau carries out CCM in order to meet its goal of improving the 2020 Census.

For example, in our 2008 report, we recommended that the Bureau provide decision points and plans for evaluating CCM. In September 2009, the Bureau finalized its list of 22 planned evaluations for the 2010 Census, which included five that address specific methodological or procedural topics within the CCM program. However, all study plans are not due to be completed until April 2010. In addition, while the deadlines for finalizing CCM estimation methods have not yet passed, the Bureau has many of its default plans already in place. Default plans allow the Bureau to move forward on schedule even if new plans have not been developed. Table 1 shows the status of the Bureau's plans for the design of CCM in each of these areas.

Table 1. Status of the Bureau's Decisions in Key Areas of the Census Coverage Measurement Program

CCM plan area	Decision status	Decision date	Comment
Goals	Finalized	Sept. 2005	The goals have not substantially changed and are subject to refinement as research on how to meet them progresses.
Timing Of Person Interviewing	Finalized	June 2009	In 2009, the Bureau reconsidered and stayed with its earlier decision on the timing of this operation.
Of releasing results	Finalized	June 2009	The Bureau decided to move reporting forward by about 3 months from initial baseline schedule.
Estimation Methods	In progress	est. April 2010	Default plans are largely in place, but the Bureau is researching additional technical improvements.
Results to Produce By level of geography	In progress	Spring 2010	The Bureau will publicize the levels of estimates planned for below the state level.
By demographic groups	Finalized	June 2009	The Bureau plans public dissemination of the planned reporting groups in early 2010.
Evaluations Topics	Finalized	Sept. 2009	Additional studies are expected outside the formal evaluation program. The Bureau also plans a series of technical memorandums documenting CCM process and results, similar to its approach for the 2000 Census.
Study plans	In progress	est. April 2010	Subject area experts will complete study plans on a rolling basis until the deadline.
Master Trace Project	In progress	est. Sept. 2010	The Director of the Census Bureau recently initiated the Master Trace Project.

Source: GAO analysis of Bureau documentation and schedule.

Recent Changes to CCM Data Collection Plan Could Improve Quality of CCM Data

In September 2009, shortly after taking office, the Director of the Census Bureau asked the staff responsible for CCM to review its CCM design and propose specific changes that would reduce the introduction of nonsampling error—such as human errors made when recording data during interviews—into CCM and its resulting estimates. The staff proposed numerous changes intended to reduce error in collected data. They also proposed an additional research study. The Director approved all of these proposals in mid-December 2009. Key changes included:

- increasing the reinterview rates for CCM field work to improve quality assurance;
- increasing training time for short-term workers hired to conduct door-to-door visits during the Person Interviewing operation to improve interview techniques for local or other special situations due to current economic conditions (such as people who became homeless or have had to move frequently during the housing crisis);
- increasing supervisor-to-employee field staffing ratios to improve quality and monitoring of field work at each level; and
- adding a telephone-based study to collect information about how well respondents recall information about their residence and possible movement since Census Day.

In addition, the decision authorized a nearly 45 percent reduction in the CCM sample size that the Bureau believes would generate the cost savings to pay for the other changes. Our understanding of the issues suggests that these are reasonable efforts to improve survey quality. The Bureau's reduction in sample size will reduce precision of the estimates, yet the proposed changes should reduce nonsampling errors and thus provide users with more reliable estimates. For example, the Bureau expects short-term CCM workers to make fewer mistakes in identifying temporary or unconventional housing units when they have received additional training specific to their local circumstances, such as in areas with large numbers of seasonal or displaced workers.

THE BUREAU NEEDS TO TAKE ADDITIONAL ACTIONS TO IMPROVE THE USEFULNESS OF CCM

The Bureau's actions to finalize some areas of CCM program planning are important steps in the right direction. Still, in some cases, it will be important for the Bureau to take additional actions to help ensure the results of CCM are as useful as they could be to inform Bureau decisions on improving future censuses and coverage measurement efforts.

For example, the Bureau could better document how CCM results will be used as part of the planning process for the 2020 Census. Indeed, the Bureau has already begun laying the foundation for its 2020 planning efforts. These early planning efforts are described in a series of decision memorandums issued in the summer of 2009, and include milestones leading up to a census test in April 2014, descriptions of planning phases, and a list of the various organizational components that conduct the census. Although these planning documents explicitly state the importance of relying on the 2010 Census Evaluation and Testing program—an ongoing assessment effort separate from CCM that, like CCM, is designed to improve future operations—the Bureau has not yet taken similar steps to integrate the CCM program with 2020 planning. In addition, the Bureau does not have specific plans in its CCM program goals to do anything beyond producing CCM results.

Bureau officials have maintained that until it produces CCM results, it is difficult to determine how to use CCM data to improve the design of future decennials. While we agree with the Bureau that the results will determine the specifics of any potential design improvements, it is not premature to consider how the earliest results from CCM—scheduled for early 2012— could help inform early planning and decisions. Importantly, by creating a "roadmap" that describes, for example, what the Bureau might learn from CCM or how the results might feed into early 2020 Census planning, the Bureau will better ensure that there are no gaps or overlaps in the use of CCM in early 2020 planning.

The Bureau's Master Trace Project is another area where additional efforts are needed to ensure useful CCM results. The Bureau initiated the Master Trace Project in September 2009, to facilitate the use of census and CCM data for future research. Currently, Bureau data are collected and archived in different types of datasets and systems. The Master Trace Project is intended to ensure that these datasets and systems can be used together, or linked, to support detailed research into the causes of census coverage problems and facilitate research on the possible interactions of future operations. For example, a researcher might want to see if there is a relationship between the Bureau's employment practices and the magnitude of an undercount in a particular area. In so doing, the researcher may want to compare census payroll, overtime, and other human capital data to the data from that region collected and processed by census and CCM. Such datasets would not ordinarily be linked during the census.

The Bureau has not yet taken the steps needed to ensure that such research across different data systems would be possible. The Bureau held a meeting in December 2009 with staff responsible for many major decennial systems and obtained agreement about the importance of data retention for this project; however, the Bureau has not yet resolved how it would make the project happen. In particular, the Bureau has not yet completed an inventory of the census databases that might be of potential interest for future research, identified which archived versions might be most useful, or mapped out how they might be archived and linked. Until this is done, it is unclear that Bureau or other researchers will have access to census operational data that they need to fully analyze the census coverage errors that CCM may uncover. Moving forward, it will be important for the Bureau to perform the initial assessment of its data systems, identify gaps in data collection, and identify any other related steps to ensure that key data can be linked. Doing this quickly will also be important as Census 2010 is underway and it could become increasingly difficult to make changes to database structures or archival and data storage plans if the Bureau's assessments determine that changes are necessary.

A third area where the Bureau needs to do additional work is in assessing how the timing of CCM data collection might adversely affect CCM findings. When planning CCM, the Bureau faced the challenge of determining the optimal time to launch the CCM data collection operation, known as Person Interviewing (PI). If the Bureau starts PI too early, it increases the chance that it overlaps with census data collection, possibly compromising the independence of the two different operations and introducing a "contamination bias" error into CCM data. If the Bureau starts PI too late, it increases the chance that respondents will not accurately remember household information from Census Day, April 1, introducing error (known as "recall bias") in the CCM count. Both types of errors—contamination bias and recall bias—could affect the Bureau's conclusions about the accuracy of the census. An understanding of the trade-offs between these two types of biases would be important in future decisions regarding the optimal timing of PI.

In early 2009, based on concerns by the National Academy of Sciences (NAS) and other stakeholders about the relative lateness in the start date of PI and its possible impact on the quality of CCM findings, the Bureau considered whether to start PI 6 weeks earlier than planned. In June 2009, the Bureau decided to keep the originally scheduled start on August 14, 2010. Bureau memorandums and officials justified the decision largely because of concern that it was too late in the planning process to make a change in the complex CCM schedule. The memorandums cited gaps in knowledge about the impact of timing on recall bias, presented research with differing conclusions about the extent of contamination in prior census tests, and justified the recommendation to not change the start date by the operational challenges faced to make the change.

Bureau officials have also explained that the goal of using coverage measurement in 2000 to possibly adjust the census-created time pressures in 2000 that forced an early PI, and because such time pressures do not exist for PI in 2010, it is scheduled to begin more than 4 months after Census Day.

By comparison, during the 2000 Census, the Bureau launched PI in April 2000 and had completed about 99 percent of its data collection by the end of the first week of August 2000, a week earlier than the scheduled 2010 PI start date. An extensive 2000 Census evaluation found no evidence of contamination bias caused by the earlier start of PI in 2000. Related Bureau research since then has also found no significant evidence of contamination bias during census tests, although one test found that census results could be affected. Yet Bureau officials remained concerned about the possibility, since the CCM questions are similar to follow-up questions used in one of the 2010 census follow-up operations. Furthermore, parts of this census operation are new in 2010, and end later than similar operations did in 2000.

Moving forward, additional research on the trade-offs between recall bias and contamination errors could help the Bureau more fully understand the implications of choosing various start times for PI on the resulting estimates of coverage error and better determine the optimal timing of PI in future censuses. Currently, the Bureau has a telephone-based study planned in order to measure recall errors, which could provide additional information about when recall errors are more likely to occur. However, this study is limited to certain types of recall error, and the Bureau does not have an evaluation planned to measure possible contamination between the new, much later, parts of census follow-up and CCM data collection or to assess the trade-offs between the biases from starting earlier compared to starting later. Such additional study after the 2010 Census could provide the Bureau better information about the trade-offs in data quality from potential contamination and recall biases and provide a better basis for determining the optimal scheduling of coverage measurement operations.

CONCLUSIONS

Assessing the accuracy of the census is an essential step in improving current and future censuses. The Bureau has made progress on designing and planning for its CCM program and continues activity to complete the plan. Additional actions in three CCM planning areas may further improve CCM or its usefulness to the 2020 Census.

Specifically, the Bureau has stated the importance of using 2010 evaluation data such as CCM's for 2020 Census design, but has not yet taken steps to link CCM data to an improved 2020 design. If the Bureau is to best achieve its goal of using CCM to help improve the 2020 Census, it will need to integrate planning for any follow-up work on CCM results or data with the other early planning already underway for Census 2020.

Second, the Bureau has many different processes that come together in the conduct of a decennial census, and archived data on those processes could provide useful information to researchers trying to figure out what worked well and what did not. The Master Trace Project can help researchers link CCM results and data to potential design changes for Census 2020. Determining which data need to be linked or archived to enable future linkage within the project can help prevent gaps in 2010 data that might hinder the project's ability to help identify improvements for the 2020 Census.

Third, the timing of CCM's primary data collection operation—Person Interviewing—involves trade-offs between reducing contamination bias and reducing recall error that the Bureau did not have conclusive information on. Since 2010 Person Interviewing is starting 1 week after a similar operation ended in 2000, the chance of introducing recall bias errors into CCM data is higher in 2010 than it was in 2000. Although the Bureau has a study planned to measure some recall errors, there is no study planned to measure contamination between the new parts of census follow-up—which use questions similar to those asked by CCM and finish much later than follow-up did in 2000—and CCM or to assess the tradeoffs between the two types of biases in timing decisions. Targeted research after the 2010 Census on the relationship between the timing of data collection and the trade-offs between these types of errors before the 2020 Census and its coverage measurement efforts could help the Bureau better determine the optimal timing of future data collection operations.

RECOMMENDATIONS FOR EXECUTIVE ACTION

We recommend that the Secretary of Commerce require the Director of the U.S. Census Bureau to take the following three actions to improve the usefulness of CCM for 2020: To help the Bureau achieve its goal of using CCM to improve the 2020 Census, better document links between the 2010 CCM program and 2020 Census planning, integrating the goal of using the CCM program to improve Census 2020, such as with CCM results and data, into those broader plans for 2020.

To ensure that Bureau datasets from the 2010 Census can be used with other Bureau datasets to support research that could improve the census and CCM, complete the Master Trace Project's assessment of how key census and CCM data systems are, or can be, linked to each other; identify any potential data gaps; and identify other related steps for future action.

To help the Bureau better determine the optimal timing of future coverage measurement data collection, fully assess the trade-offs between starting the data collection earlier, with the possibility of introducing contamination errors, and starting later, with the possibility of introducing recall errors.

AGENCY COMMENTS AND OUR EVALUATION

The Secretary of Commerce provided written comments on a draft of this report on April 5, 2010. The comments are reprinted in appendix I. Commerce generally agreed with the overall findings and recommendations and appreciated our efforts in helping the Census Bureau develop a successful evaluation plan for the 2020 Census. Commerce also provided additional information and comments on certain statements and conclusions in the report.

With respect to our second recommendation to complete the Master Trace Project's assessment of linking key census and CCM data systems, to identify any potential data gaps, and to identify other related steps for future action, Commerce maintained that it would be taking action to preserve adequate documentation and maximize the amount of data retained from each major decennial system. We commend the Bureau for committing to these steps and encourage its follow-through on them and its identification of remaining data gaps and additional steps needed.

With respect to our third recommendation to fully assess the trade-offs between two types of error related to starting CCM data collection either earlier or later relative to Census Day, Commerce responded that (1) it is too late to create a new study for 2010 Census; (2) it considers a Bureau contamination study from 2000 to be definitive; and (3) it has recently developed a study on recall bias to try to measure some of the effects of scheduling CCM data collection at various periods of time following the census enumeration. We agree that it is too late to attempt any additional unplanned data collection during the 2010 Census, and we revised our discussion to clarify our intent that the recommended research be conducted after the 2010 Census. We also recognize the thoroughness of the 2000 contamination study the Bureau cites, commend the Bureau on undertaking additional study of recall bias, and look forward to reviewing its study plans when they are available. However, we recommended research comparing trade-offs between the two types of errors at a variety of start dates for CCM data collection—something the 2000 study did not discuss and something it is unclear that a study of only recall bias will achieve. Furthermore as we discussed in our draft report, the Bureau expressed concerns over possible contamination between CCM and new parts of census follow-up in 2010—parts that were introduced after the 2000 study and that were not included in the scope of the 2000 study. We clarified our discussion of this in the report to better focus on the need for research that relates the trade-offs between the two types of error at different timing of data collection.

Commerce provided additional information that in response to advice from various advisory panels and after additional research, it would soon make public its proposed geographic levels for CCM estimates. We reflected this decision in table 1 of our report.

Finally, Commerce provided additional information about its plans to produce highly technical documentation of the results of CCM estimation including modeling, missing data, and errors in the estimates in a series of memorandums as it did for Census 2000. We reflected this decision in table 1 of this report.

APPENDIX I: COMMENTS FROM THE DEPARTMENT OF COMMERCE

April 5, 2010

Mr. Robert Goldenkoff
Director
Strategic Issues
U.S. Government Accountability Office
Washington, DC 20548

Dear Mr. Goldenkoff:

The Department of Commerce (Department) appreciates the opportunity to comment on the U.S. Government Accountability Office's draft report entitled *"2010 Census: Plans for Census Coverage Measurement Are on Track, but Additional Steps Will Improve Its Usefulness"* (GAO-10-324). The Department's comments on this report are enclosed.

Sincerely,

Gary Locke

Enclosure

U.S. Department of Commerce
Comments on the
United States Government Accountability Office
Draft Report Entitled *2010 Census: Plans for Census Coverage Measurement Are on Track, but Additional Steps Will Improve Its Usefulness*
GAO 10-324
March 2010

The U.S. Census Bureau would like to thank the Government Accountability Office (GAO) for its efforts in examining the 2010 Census Coverage Measurement (CCM) program plans for assessing the accuracy of the 2010 Census, and for the opportunity to comment on the observations and recommendations in this report.

We have no fundamental disagreements with the overall findings or the recommendations regarding improvements in our evaluation processes for the 2020 Census cycle. We do, however, offer the following comments on certain statements and conclusions in this report.

- Page 6, second bullet: "The Bureau will not decide the level of geography for which to release estimates before knowing the quality of the results."

    Census Bureau response: In response to advice from various advisory panels and after additional research in the spring of 2010, we will make public the proposed geographic levels of the estimates below the state level (already planned).

- Page 6, third bullet: "Additional studies are expected outside the formal evaluation program."

Census Bureau response: In response to advice from various advisory panels and after additional research in the spring of 2010, we will make public the proposed geographic levels of the estimates below the state level (already planned).

- Page 6, third bullet: "Additional studies are expected outside the formal evaluation program."

Census Bureau response: We have recently developed a study on recall bias to try to measure some of the effects of scheduling Person Interviewing at various periods of time following the census enumeration. This study is not yet part of the formal evaluation program. In addition, to document the results from CCM estimation—including modeling, missing data, and errors in the estimates—we will produce a series of memorandums. The results will not come from experiments or evaluations but will be based on actual data and estimates from the CCM. This highly technical documentation is similar to our approach for Census 2000.

- Page 9: "The Bureau's Master Trace Project is another area where additional efforts are needed to ensure useful CCM results."

Census Bureau response: The Census Bureau is currently taking actions in accordance with GAO's recommendation on retaining and linking 2010 Census data (including CCM data) for purposes of analysis and 2020 census planning. In addition to preserving adequate documentation, the Census Bureau's immediate focus is to maximize the amount of data retained from each major decennial system. As the Census Bureau can strategically leverage the time of key staff members during the implementation of the 2010 Census, the polishing of data documentation and the development of guidelines on how to link data from different decennial systems will take final form. As part of this process, we plan to save all data collection and processing files from the CCM.

- Page 11: "Yet Bureau officials remained concerned about the possibility [of contamination], since the CCM questions are similar to follow-up questions used in one of the 2010 follow-up operations."

Census Bureau response: Parts of this census operation are new in 2010 and end later than similar operations did in 2000. Their timing also pushed back the start of Person Interviewing.

- Page 13: "To help the Bureau ... fully assess the tradeoffs between starting the data collection earlier ... and starting later ...."

Census Bureau response: We ran a careful, and what we consider definitive, contamination study in 2000. We cannot create a new study for the 2010 Census now, as it's too late,. We would have had to create a separate Person Interviewing panel to undergo an early interview and measure its contamination. For reasons of cost and response burden, we do not want to repeat studies unless we expect to learn more from them. Furthermore, we would not have had an instrument ready to conduct a contamination test.

In conclusion, we acknowledge the GAO's extensive work in reviewing these activities, and we appreciate its ongoing efforts to help us develop a successful evaluation plan for the 2020 Census.

End Notes

[1] GAO-08-414, 2010 CENSUS: Bureau Needs to Specify How It Will Assess Coverage Follow-up Techniques and When It Will Produce Coverage Measurement Results (April 25, 2008).

[2] Robert M. Bell and Michael L. Cohen, eds., Coverage Measurement in the 2010 Census (Washington, D.C.: The National Academies Press, 2009).

[3] Dep't of Commerce v. U.S. House of Representatives, 525 U.S. 316 (1999) (citing 13 U.S.C. §195.

INDEX

A

access, 21, 50, 87, 90, 94, 142, 154
accountability, 39, 57, 60, 61, 63
activity level, 103
adjustment, 14, 15, 16, 149
agencies, 20, 35, 39, 56, 61, 140
American Recovery and Reinvestment Act of 2009, 79, 114
assessment, 14, 55, 59, 113, 121, 123, 153, 154, 157
assignment area, 33, 45, 51
audit, 37, 67, 78, 114, 133, 148
automate, 2, 3, 6
automation, 5
autonomy, 28
awareness, 16, 17, 35, 82, 83, 85, 86, 104

B

Be Counted/Questionnaire Assistance Center (QAC), viii, 73, 74, 75, 76, 77, 78, 79, 80, 98, 99, 100, 101, 102, 103, 104, 106, 110
benefits, 22, 60, 61, 62, 82, 84, 117, 131
bias, 13, 14, 21, 22, 55, 146, 150, 154, 155, 156, 158
Blacks, 11, 12, 13, 16
Bureau of the Census, vii, 1, 3, 4, 12, 21, 22, 23, 24, 25, 26, 27
businesses, 17, 130, 132, 139

C

candidates, 17, 41, 64
Census Coverage Measurement program (CCM), ix, 13, 14, 16, 22, 33, 36, 54, 145, 146, 147, 148, 149, 150, 151, 152, 153, 154, 155, 156, 157, 158
census forms, vii, viii, 1, 2, 3, 4, 5, 10, 18, 31, 35, 36, 37, 55, 64, 87, 92, 109, 112, 129, 132, 133
challenges, 6, 21, 32, 34, 35, 38, 39, 45, 51, 58, 74, 75, 80, 85, 87, 88, 89, 92, 94, 96, 98, 104, 124, 130, 135, 136, 138, 140, 142, 155
children, 17, 76, 113, 116, 119, 135
civil rights, 130, 138
collaboration, 36, 56, 67
college students, 50, 120
commercial, 122, 123, 124
communication, 77, 87, 88, 90, 92, 95, 105, 124, 125, 126, 142
communities, 60, 87, 91, 94, 109, 130, 142
community, 17, 18, 22, 44, 76, 80, 87, 89, 90, 93, 142
complexity, viii, 54, 111, 113, 131, 148
compliance, 3, 22, 130, 138
conference, 87, 109
confidentiality, 57, 87, 140

Index

Congress, ix, 3, 6, 7, 15, 19, 20, 21, 22, 23, 24, 25, 26, 27, 28, 34, 35, 36, 56, 58, 59, 62, 65, 76, 109, 114, 131, 145, 147
Constitution, 2, 137
contamination, 14, 55, 146, 154, 155, 156, 157, 158
contingency, 7, 24, 42, 83, 117, 118, 126
cooperation, 17, 41, 88, 142, 143
coordination, 74, 87, 88, 89, 92, 104, 105
cost saving, 54, 117, 124, 152
Coverage Follow-up (CFU), viii, 111, 112, 113, 114, 116, 118, 119, 120, 121, 122, 123, 124, 128, 160
CRS report, 20
culture, 32, 39, 62, 67

D

data collection, vii, 14, 31, 33, 49, 55, 57, 65, 77, 119, 123, 132, 140, 154, 155, 156, 157, 158
data processing, 45, 112, 118
database, 74, 85, 86, 90, 92, 104, 105, 109, 122, 123, 124, 131, 140, 147, 154
demographic change, 139
demographic characteristics, 112, 121, 123, 125, 134
demographic data, 11
Department of Commerce, 3, 15, 20, 23, 24, 26, 32, 37, 62, 64, 68, 77, 79, 97, 106, 107, 109, 126, 146, 147, 159
directors, 60, 61
dissatisfaction, 48, 75, 88, 89, 97, 103
distribution, 3, 78, 92, 138
District of Columbia, 5, 20, 41, 67
diversity, 35, 36, 65, 77, 78, 133
DOC, 3, 6, 28
draft, 7, 37, 63, 69, 79, 106, 126, 128, 157, 158

E

election, 130, 139
English language proficiency, 10

environment, 8, 39, 71, 136
ethnic groups, 78, 85, 89
ethnicity, 2, 5, 13
evidence, 37, 57, 67, 78, 79, 114, 133, 148, 149, 155

F

families, 10, 119
FBI, 19, 33, 47, 48, 70
federal aid, 37, 131
federal assistance, 76, 130, 131, 138, 147
Federal Bureau of Investigation, 19, 33, 47, 70
federal funds, 16, 149
federal government, 39, 70
Federal Register, 27
Field Verification (FV), viii, 111, 112, 113, 114, 115, 116, 117, 118, 119, 124, 126
fingerprints, 19, 47, 48, 63, 64, 65, 70
fiscal year 2009, 130, 138
Fourteenth Amendment, 2
funding, 20, 85, 87, 118, 122
funds, 3, 24, 74, 105, 109, 114, 138

G

geography, 21, 44, 151
governments, 17, 130, 139
grants, 130, 138
Great Depression, 23
guidance, 59, 74, 75, 87, 93, 94, 97, 98, 100, 102, 103, 104, 106, 132
Gulf Coast, 18, 37, 132, 133

H

hard-to-count (HTC), viii, 36, 73, 74, 75, 76, 77, 78, 79, 82, 87, 90, 91, 92, 94, 102, 104, 105, 106, 140
hiring, 54, 62, 74, 91
Hispanics, 13, 16, 84, 123
homelessness, 14, 78
homes, 18, 76, 135, 140

hourly wage, 56
House, 2, 3, 4, 6, 14, 15, 16, 20, 21, 22, 23, 25, 26, 27, 28, 34, 76, 130, 131, 137, 149, 161
House of Representatives, 3, 34, 76, 137, 149, 161
housing, viii, 2, 4, 5, 9, 13, 18, 22, 23, 24, 25, 33, 36, 37, 39, 40, 41, 43, 46, 51, 52, 53, 54, 55, 56, 57, 66, 76, 80, 81, 92, 104, 110, 111, 113, 117, 129, 131, 132, 133, 134, 135, 143, 149, 152
Housing and Urban Development, 119
human capital, 36, 67, 154

I

immigration, 11, 140, 149
improvements, 8, 14, 90, 92, 121, 153, 156
income, 10, 123, 138
independence, 13, 14, 55, 150, 154
individuals, viii, 60, 63, 73, 76, 82, 92, 94, 95, 96, 102, 130, 131, 133, 134, 138
information technology, 7, 9, 32, 33, 34, 65, 113, 117, 137
infrastructure, 7, 8, 16, 58, 60, 62
international migration, 10, 11
invasion of privacy, 81
investment, 35, 49, 52, 56, 71, 85, 130, 131, 147
investments, 51, 61
issues, vii, 2, 7, 8, 16, 31, 32, 38, 49, 56, 57, 93, 98, 104, 106, 142, 152

K

kindergarten, 17

L

labor force, 139
labor market, 41
language barrier, 131, 140
languages, 18, 74, 81, 83, 86, 87, 98, 99
laws, 130, 138

lesson plan, 17
life cycle, 34, 60
living arrangements, 38
local census offices (LCO), 4, 9, 32, 33, 36, 43, 45, 46, 47, 48, 50, 51, 53, 65, 66, 74, 77, 78, 79, 85, 88, 89, 92, 94, 99, 100, 109, 132, 136, 137, 140, 141, 142
local community, 87
local conditions, 95
local government, 2, 17, 37, 76, 93, 131, 139, 147
local labor markets, 137

M

Matching Review and Coding System, 33, 66
media, 17, 57, 60, 63, 76, 77, 78, 79, 80, 81, 82, 83, 84, 85, 104, 105, 124
media messages, 83
Medicaid, 130, 138
Medicare, 11
methodology, 13, 22, 35, 36, 64, 150
migrants, 10, 77, 80, 115
migration, 11
military, 24, 27, 121
minorities, viii, 2, 10, 73, 113, 123
minority groups, 16, 122, 134
mission, 52, 58, 70
modifications, 62, 64
momentum, 59
music, 139

N

NAS, 148, 155
National Processing Center, 33, 48
new media, 84
nonprofit organizations, 35
nonresponse follow-up (NRFU), vii, viii, 2, 4, 5, 6, 8, 9, 17, 19, 21, 24, 31, 32, 33, 36, 39, 41, 42, 43, 44, 45, 46, 47, 48, 49, 50, 51, 52, 53, 58, 62, 63, 64, 65, 66, 70,

Index

88, 129, 130, 131, 132, 133, 134, 135, 136, 140, 141, 142, 143
nursing home, 18, 24, 27, 37, 112, 116, 133

O

Obama Administration, 15, 20
Office of Management and Budget, 27, 59
officials, viii, ix, 15, 17, 27, 36, 46, 52, 53, 61, 65, 66, 67, 74, 77, 78, 79, 89, 90, 91, 92, 94, 95, 96, 97, 98, 102, 111, 114, 117, 121, 122, 132, 146, 148, 153, 155
opportunity costs, 103
organizational culture, 56
outreach, viii, 41, 73, 74, 76, 77, 78, 79, 81, 82, 84, 87, 90, 104, 105, 109, 136
outreach programs, viii, 73

P

Paper-Based Operations Control System, 8, 33, 45, 65
Patriot Act, 140, 143
payroll, 98, 154
platform, 57
policy, 32, 51, 56, 63, 96
political leaders, 60
politics, 20, 26
polling, 83
population, vii, viii, 1, 2, 3, 4, 10, 11, 12, 13, 14, 15, 21, 22, 23, 25, 34, 35, 37, 39, 52, 54, 55, 56, 57, 62, 76, 78, 79, 80, 82, 83, 85, 93, 97, 104, 105, 108, 111, 113, 115, 121, 130, 131, 134, 135, 137, 138, 139, 140, 147, 148, 149, 150
population group, 22, 80, 113
population size, 3, 10
poverty, 131, 140
primary data, 156
prisons, 18, 24, 27, 37, 133
private schools, 18
project, 59, 154, 156
prototypes, 6
public safety, 20

Q

quality assurance, 13, 93, 99, 118, 141, 152
query, 16
questionnaire, 2, 3, 4, 5, 10, 18, 35, 38, 41, 43, 52, 62, 65, 66, 70, 80, 93, 96, 115, 119, 133, 136, 143

R

race, 2, 5, 13, 45, 121, 135
recall information, 14, 152
recruiting, 4, 17, 35, 41, 63, 64, 87, 88, 91, 136, 137
redistricting, 3, 4, 15, 16, 137, 149
regional unemployment, 63
regression analysis, 70
regression model, 66
reliability, 9, 37, 49, 50, 66, 130, 137
requirements, 7, 51, 60, 90
researchers, 10, 154, 156
resources, 35, 39, 60, 83, 91, 104, 105, 112, 121
response, 9, 16, 19, 22, 23, 24, 32, 35, 38, 39, 40, 41, 43, 45, 46, 53, 55, 56, 57, 65, 70, 74, 78, 79, 81, 83, 84, 85, 90, 92, 97, 104, 105, 106, 115, 117, 121, 122, 130, 132, 134, 135, 136, 143, 158
restrictions, 50
risk management, 39, 51
rules, 10, 123, 125
rural areas, 44, 132, 133
rural population, 65

S

schedule delays, 49
school, 27, 56, 83, 139
scope, 36, 112, 114, 119, 120, 131, 158
Secretary of Commerce, 3, 26, 37, 63, 79, 105, 106, 112, 125, 126, 149, 157
Senate, 3, 15, 20, 21, 26, 28, 34, 60, 61, 75
service provider, viii, 73, 75, 92, 94, 96

Service-Based Enumeration (SBE), viii, 73, 74, 75, 76, 77, 78, 79, 80, 92, 93, 94, 95, 96, 97, 103, 104, 106, 109
shelter, 96, 97
social services, 138
society, 2, 10, 131
software, 6, 8, 9, 49, 50, 63, 137
soup kitchens, viii, 18, 73
staffing, ix, 14, 32, 39, 41, 53, 62, 74, 75, 97, 99, 103, 104, 106, 109, 129, 130, 132, 135, 136, 137, 142, 152
stakeholders, 35, 36, 56, 57, 58, 59, 60, 61, 62, 63, 65, 155
state legislatures, 138
statistics, 11
storage, 147, 154
strategic planning, 56
structure, 56, 58, 59, 79, 87, 88, 89, 90
subgroups, 76, 135
Supreme Court, 14, 15, 138, 149

T

tangible benefits, 80
target, 71, 74, 76, 77, 80, 81, 104, 118, 122, 136, 139
target population, 104
tax collection, 140
technical comments, 37, 64, 133
techniques, 54, 63, 152
technology, 39, 57, 94, 112, 125, 126
telecommunications, 124
telephone numbers, 112, 113, 122, 123, 124, 125
tenure, 5, 33, 60, 61
testing, 7, 8, 9, 17, 24, 38, 49, 51, 56, 58, 59, 60, 114, 117, 124

time pressure, 155
total costs, 117
trade, 55, 58, 124, 147, 154, 155, 156, 157, 158
trade-off, 55, 58, 124, 147, 154, 155, 156, 157, 158
training, 13, 17, 19, 47, 48, 52, 54, 63, 64, 65, 75, 86, 87, 88, 92, 93, 95, 97, 98, 103, 105, 117, 138, 152

U

U.S. Department of Commerce, 23, 24, 27
U.S. Secretary of Commerce, 28
unemployment rate, 44
urban areas, 36, 78

V

vacant/delete check (VDC), 32, 33, 36, 52, 53, 62, 63, 65, 66
value-added goods, 86
vision, 58, 61
vote, 138
voting, 80, 131

W

White House, 20, 26, 28
workers, 2, 4, 9, 13, 18, 19, 24, 36, 42, 46, 48, 63, 64, 77, 80, 92, 95, 109, 115, 152
workload, viii, 4, 8, 39, 41, 43, 46, 48, 50, 53, 62, 63, 66, 70, 85, 93, 97, 99, 117, 118, 124, 126, 129, 130, 132, 134, 135, 137, 140, 141, 142, 143